Glen points out in his new _____ _____ a
burden for evangelism, bu_____ _____ l
delight in sharing God's l_____ _____ we understand the love God has for us, we will not just feel a duty
to help others, but we will have a heartfelt desire to actually show the love of God to others. Take it outside of the
four walls of the church and let the love of God infect
people. But we have to be in love with God first. His
book teaches us how to accomplish this. Glen has such
a gift of seeing the bottom line and getting across to us
truths many have not grasped. A most-needed and excel-
lent book for all!

—BILL WIESE
AUTHOR OF THE *NEW YORK TIMES* BEST-SELLING BOOK
23 MINUTES IN HELL

Glen Berteau is an apostolic leader who has incredible
insight and has seen amazing results through his life. He
literally has seen hundreds of thousands of people come
to know Christ and has been used to impact a city and
build a kingdom church. Glen has been a powerful voice
into my life personally and our church and movement at
Planetshakers. Glen is a man of conviction and has great
authority to bring change and breakthrough.

Glen's life has seen growth and breakthrough wherever
he has gone. This book will inspire, empower, impact, and
bring breakthrough to your life. Glen holds no punches,
and in his frank and insightful communication he will
leave you wanting more of God in your life.

—PASTOR RUSSELL EVANS
PLANETSHAKERS, AUSTRALIA

The voice and gift of Glen Berteau have affected an international audience. His unique ability to understand the Word of God and to explicate its intricacies to the hearer is remarkable. When reading this book, you will see yourself as if looking into a mirror, beholding the beauty that is in you and the beauty that is in the body of Christ. Read it. Allow its message to pervade your thinking. Your life will be the better for it.

—STEVE K. MUNSEY, PHD
SENIOR PASTOR OF FAMILY CHRISTIAN CENTER
MUNSTER, INDIANA

My dear friend, mentor, and coach has done it again! Pastor Glen Berteau has captured the heart of God in *Christianity to Go*. I personally have been deeply impacted by seeing this message at work in the city of Modesto, California, through Pastor Glen Berteau's church "The House." The message within the pages of this book is a modern-day "Sermon on the Mt. of Olives"! You will be personally stirred to get out of the mirror and look out the window to see the lost, hear the lost, and encounter the lost! We must leave our sightly cathedrals and boardrooms and be Jesus with flesh on. This is not a "how-to" book, but rather it's a "what if?" This book will awaken you to realize that you are God's billboard! We are not called to be in sales but rather advertising! This book has challenged me to realize that I am the miracle others need to see! My heart has been so stirred by this message to rightly represent our King with compassion, love, and freedom.

—PATRICK SCHATZLINE
EVANGELIST AND PRESIDENT OF MERCY SEAT MINISTRIES
AUTHOR OF *WHY IS GOD SO MAD AT ME?*

Jesus paid a huge price for all to be saved, and He left us the privilege of telling those who have never heard this good news. Glen Berteau's book conveys the strategies of a church that sees over 10,000 people saved each year. I respect his ministry, his message, and his ability to win souls. You will catch his passion for the lost as you immerse yourself in this message.

—JOHN BEVERE
AUTHOR / SPEAKER
MESSENGER INTERNATIONAL
COLORADO / AUSTRALIA / UNITED KINGDOM

I love Pastor Glen Berteau. He challenges me—not in a way to make me feel small but in a way that makes me want to be larger. He does it again in *Christianity to Go*, reminding me that the greatest source of touching a world in need of healing on every level is not a program rather the overflow of your life—when you can't help but help! This book will surround you with your destiny so your talk becomes your walk. You'll want to get a copy of this book for all you love.

—DR. SAMUEL R. CHAND
AUTHOR OF *CRACKING YOUR CHURCH'S CULTURE CODE*
WWW.SAMCHAND.COM

To Mickey!

Christianity
TO GO

Witness,

GLEN BERTEAU

PASSIO
THE ART OF AUTHENTIC FAITH

CHRISTIANITY TO GO by Glen Berteau
Published by Passio
Charisma Media/Charisma House Book Group
600 Rinehart Road
Lake Mary, Florida 32746
www.charismahouse.com

Cover design by Lisa Rae Cox
Design Director: Bill Johnson

Names and details of the stories in this book have been changed to protect the privacy of the individuals.

Visit the author's website at www.glenberteau.com.

Library of Congress Control Number: 2013908886
International Standard Book Number: 978-1-62136-292-0
E-book ISBN: 978-1-62136-293-7

While the author has made every effort to provide accurate telephone numbers and Internet addresses at the time of publication, neither the publisher nor the author assumes any responsibility for errors or for changes that occur after publication.

First edition

13 14 15 16 17 — 9 8 7 6 5 4 3 2 1
Printed in the United States of America

This book is dedicated to my family, who live every day for winning souls.

To my beautiful wife, Deborah. Without your love, support (friendship), and prayer covering I would not be the man I am today. I will love you always. You are the ultimate prayer warrior!

To my three children and their spouses—Kelli and Michael Williams, Christy and Jeremy Johnson, and Micah and Lindsey Berteau. It is a joy and a privilege to have children who love God and family. I am honored to share the call of God with you.

To my grandchildren: Jotham and Zoe Williams and Lyric and Brave Johnson. You bring a new kind of joy to my life. I look forward to watching you grow and become who God has called you to be.

I am a blessed man with a supernatural family.

CONTENTS

INTRODUCTION

THIS ISN'T A book about evangelism. It's much more than that. I'm not going to wag my finger at you to make you feel so guilty that you talk to your neighbor about Jesus. I'm not going to heap shame on you and use a ton of oughts and shoulds to bludgeon you into obedience to share your faith. This book also isn't about techniques of how to share the gospel, and it's not full of sociological studies of our culture. Tools, techniques, and studies have value, but they aren't the focus of what I'm trying to communicate.

Church buildings are important. They give us a place where we can gather, but they're just buildings. They're not the real church. Years ago when Elvis Presley was the biggest star on earth, his concerts were packed with fans. After his last song people often stayed around hoping for another encore or at least a glimpse of him. They stayed so long that concert promoters started making an announcement a few minutes after his last song: "Elvis has left the building!" It was a signal for everybody to go home—but even more the promoters wanted people to go out and tell their friends all about the concert.

In the same way it's time for the church to leave the building. It's important for us to gather to worship and learn truths from the Bible, but concerts and church services are momentary, temporary events. Real life happens when we leave the building. Some churches focus all their attention on what happens for an hour or so on Sunday morning. There's more to spiritual life than that—much more. Our impact shouldn't *end* when we walk out the doors of the church. It should *begin* at that moment. I'm not the pastor of a church; I'm the pastor of a city. Every corner of our community is where I serve, love, and care. Every believer has a spiritual role in their city or town too.

This book is about beauty. The people who are effective in leading people to saving faith are beautiful—maybe not on the outside, but certainly on the inside. They're in love with Jesus. They live with a sense of wonder that He loves them, accepts them, and even delights in them. The sheer joy of being loved overflows like a flood from their hearts to others. As they go through their day, they don't *do* evangelism; they *are* lovers.

> "Your fame soon spread throughout the world because of your beauty. I dressed you in my splendor and perfected your beauty" (Ezek. 16:14).

People who delight in the grace of God smell great. It's as if they're wearing the most lovely perfume or cologne. Paul told the Corinthians, "But thanks be to God, who always leads us in triumphal procession in Christ and through us spreads everywhere the fragrance of the knowledge of him" (2 Cor. 2:14, NIV).

Our lives are full of responsibilities and distractions. We're busy and have our own problems to deal with, but when the magnificence of God's love captures our hearts, our priorities change. King David was busy too. He had a whole kingdom to run. Maybe he did the dishes too. He had tons of responsibilities, but one thing was at the top of his list. He wrote, "The one thing I ask of the Lord—the thing I seek most—is to live in the house of the Lord all the days of my life, delighting in the Lord's perfections and meditating in his Temple" (Ps. 27:4). Delighting in the Lord was a priority for King David, and it still is for us.

"Delighting in the Lord's perfections." The NIV reads, "To gaze upon the beauty of the Lord." Is the Lord beautiful to you? Is He beautiful to me? If we find Him beautiful, we'll delight in Him and His Spirit will transform us from the inside out. The Christian life won't be a grind. Yes, we still obey, but we don't do so to earn points with God. We obey because *we want to please the One who delights us*—the way young lovers delight to please each other, or a beloved son or daughter finds pleasure in bringing a smile to a parent's face.

When Jesus's love floods our hearts, we won't see evangelism as a Christian duty we'd better perform...or else. The love of God overflows from us. We love the people around us, and we want them to experience God's kindness, power, and forgiveness too. It's as simple—and as profound—as that.

When we find God to be beautiful, He makes us beautiful. Today we marvel at airbrushed beauty of models and movie stars. The beauty God gives us is even more spectacular! It doesn't breed competition and jealousy. Instead, it attracts people to God. The Lord told the people of Israel, "Your fame soon spread throughout the world because of your beauty. I dressed you in my splendor and perfected your beauty" (Ezek. 16:14).

If you think this book is going to give you new techniques you can use to share your faith, you will be disappointed. But if you want "to know this love [of Christ] that surpasses knowledge" (Eph. 3:19, NIV) and have His love ooze out of every pore, keep reading. That's what real evangelism is all about.

Jesus has made you incredibly beautiful by clothing you with love, joy, and spiritual strength. Get up and leave the building. People are waiting for you to show them your beauty because your beauty points them to Jesus.

Let me begin with the story of how God used a friend's persistent love to draw me to Himself, and then I'll tell about my first experiences of sharing the beauty of Jesus with some very strange people.

one

BOOM BOOM

L IKE EVERY PERSON who is amazed at the grace of
God, I believe my story of coming to faith in Jesus
Christ is the *second* greatest story ever told. If there
was ever a least likely candidate for becoming a Christian,
I think I qualify for that label. Let me tell you why.

I'm from the deepest part of the "deep South"—born in
New Orleans and raised in Baton Rouge. Most holidays
were with family members, with a lot of people marrying
family members. We didn't have normal parties; we had
the biggest, annual blowout party in the known world:
Mardi Gras.

The food in that part of Louisiana is spicy... and really
good. In fact, when I was a baby, my mother put Tabasco
sauce in my bottle. And we didn't have to go far for
dinner. We could go down to the ditch next to the road,
grab some crawfish, and bring them back to the house to
cook them in an *étouffée*, which is a Cajun stew of shell-
fish or chicken served over rice. Some of my relatives lived
so far in the sticks they drove toward town to go hunting.
The animals lived closer than they did.

As I grew up, my parents didn't think twice about

"corporal punishment." They hadn't read modern books on child psychology and believed in "blackout" instead of "time-out." I was sixteen before I knew a belt was a piece of clothing; I thought it was a weapon of mass destruction. When I misbehaved at McDonald's, my dad would say, "Son, if you don't behave, I'm gonna supersize your backside!"

In our family, as well as throughout most of the South, people express affection by touching. People hug friends at the grocery store, men shake hands with every other man they see, and aunts, mothers, and cousins kiss every relative. At family reunions people look like victims from an explosion at a lipstick factory!

When I was in the fourth grade, I started playing pee wee football. My dad loved football, and he was eager for me to suit up and play. It was a lot of fun, but football is more than a game in Louisiana—it's a religion. Just up the road are the LSU Tigers. A game at Tiger Stadium (sometimes called "Death Valley" by losing opponents) on a Saturday night is a memorable experience, especially for the visiting team. The cheerleaders position Mike, their live Bengal tiger, at the visiting team's entrance so he can roar at them when they run out on the field. Intimidating? You bet!

As a child I wasn't very big, but I had another quality that matters on the football field. I was fast. My coaches noticed that I could outrun every player on defense, so they called a lot of plays to give me the ball. Every year other boys got bigger and I got faster. By the time I was in high school, I was one of the top running backs in the state. In fact, a number of universities came to our school to recruit me. At the time I wanted to go to college, and

I was well aware that my family couldn't afford to send me. My dad had lost his job working at an oil refinery, so times were tough. I needed a scholarship, and football was the ticket.

When I was a senior in high school, I was a scoring machine. We were the "Buccaneers," and the cheerleaders celebrated every touchdown by firing a canon. I scored at least two touchdowns in every game. The canon went off so often the crowd started calling me "Boom Boom." Soon the local newspaper picked it up and wrote headlines like, "Boom Boom Berteau Leads the Buccaneers to Another Win." By the end of the year I was a high school All-American and was chosen as one of the five best players in the state. A lot of Southern football royalty, including Southeastern Conference coaches, showed up at our games to watch me play.

After the football season I received a lot of scholarship offers. I didn't want to stay near home, so LSU was out of the picture. About that time I looked at the most recent issue of *Sports Illustrated*. On the cover was a picture of Terry Bradshaw, the superstar quarterback from Louisiana Tech. He was the top draft pick that year for the Pittsburgh Steelers. About two hours later I got a phone call. The person asked, "Is Boom Boom there?"

I answered, "This is Glen. They call me Boom Boom."

The voice said calmly, "This is Terry Bradshaw. I want to talk to you about coming to Louisiana Tech. I think you'd like it here."

I covered the phone and turned to my dad, "Dad! You won't believe it. This is Terry Bradshaw!"

I don't know if Terry said anything when I was talking to my father, but when I listened again, he said, "I'd like for you to come up to the campus this weekend so we can talk. Can you come?"

I tried to act cool, but I think my voice betrayed my excitement. "Yeah, I'll check my schedule. Uh, yeah, I think I can make it."

Ruston, Louisiana, is in the northern part of the state— far enough away from Baton Rouge. I was very impressed with the school, the football program, and especially meeting Terry Bradshaw. I signed a four-year scholarship and began my college career.

I loved being a college football player. I partied, played the guitar, and knocked heads with the defense. Some of the players and other students invited me to go to church with them from time to time, but I wasn't interested. Church seemed, well, boring and irrelevant. The music was painfully repetitive, and I didn't give a flip about Easter productions. The Christmas pageant sounded like a prison sentence, and the sermons made my most boring college classes seem like a day at Disney World. I'd grown up around a lot of nominal Christians, and it seemed they couldn't decide if God made any difference to them at all. To me church was like a bunch of somber people keeping score with rules nobody wanted to follow. I didn't want any part of it.

"BOOM BOOM, ARE YOU SAVED?"

Music was fun and exciting to me. I played the guitar, and I'd graduated from the Beatles to Jimi Hendrix, Led Zeppelin, Cream, and Deep Purple. Music had meaning. It was relevant, and it moved my soul.

The school gave a football scholarship to a young man named Denny Duron. I heard he was a good player, and

I looked forward to being on the team with him. I had no idea that Denny's father was a Pentecostal preacher, his mother was a Pentecostal preacher, and Denny was a Pentecostal preacher too. After we met and he began telling me his story, he said he had turned down Bible college so he could attend Louisiana Tech. He wanted to rub shoulders with people who needed to know God. I didn't know how that made any difference to me, but I could tell he was a young man with a purpose.

After a few days Denny said he wanted to talk to me, so I invited him to my dorm room. When he walked in, he looked around. My room was decked out in vintage Jimi Hendrix regalia: posters, amps, a rock guitar, the whole works. The first thing he said was, "Boom Boom, are you saved?"

I answered, "From what?"

He asked again, "Are you a Christian?"

I was confused. Wasn't everybody a Christian? I mean, I grew up in Louisiana. I wasn't a Buddhist, was I? Heck, no. It took a few seconds for me to figure out how to answer him, but I finally said, "I'm a Catholic."

Somehow my answer wasn't good enough for him. He then asked, "Are you born again?"

I'd heard that term somewhere before—or more likely, I'd read it on a highway overpass. I answered, "I'm Roman Catholic."

He didn't give up. "Let me ask it this way: Have you confessed with your mouth and believed in your heart that Jesus is your Savior?"

OK, that was enough. Now Denny was getting really strange. I had no idea what he was talking about. The only dots I could connect was that confession had something to do with telling a priest all the sins you'd committed that week—and I wasn't about to tell Denny about my sins! I decided to turn the tables. I asked, "Hey, are you some kind of preacher or priest, 'cause if you are..."

Without blinking, Denny nodded and explained, "Yes. Yes, I'm a preacher."

I interrupted and snapped at him, "Well, I'm not. In fact, I don't go to church. I don't like church, and I don't need church. I can sleep better in my bed. I don't want to hear any more about it!"

The odd thing is that Denny didn't look angry or offended by my outburst. He thanked me for listening—which is really strange, because I didn't really listen at all—and he walked down the hall to his room. I assumed that was the end of it. Denny Duron now knew better than to talk to me about God.

A week or so later in a football team meeting Denny got up at the end and announced that he was having a Bible study in his room on Wednesday nights. He invited everyone to come. When he sat down, I got up and invited people to join me at a local club on that Friday night. Denny had two people from the team show up Wednesday night. Most of the rest came with me on Friday to the club for music, dancing, and drinking.

Every week that year Denny made a point of inviting me to his Bible study. I laughed, and to make my point, I told him dirty jokes to see if I could get under his skin. He just smiled. It was as if he knew something I didn't.

At the end of the year everybody was packing up to leave for the summer. I told all my friends good-bye. As I was packing, I heard a knock on my dorm room door. I shouted, "Who is it?"

"It's Denny. It's urgent. I need to talk to you."

I invited him in. He blurted out, "Boom Boom, I may not be here next year."

I didn't understand. "What do you mean?" I asked. "Are you quitting the team?"

He chuckled and explained, "No, but I may be quitting earth."

I'm sure the puzzled expression on my face was priceless. He continued, "The Rapture may happen by the time the team gets together for two-a-days."

Now I was really confused. I thought he said "rafter," so I asked, "Why are you talking about the roof?"

It took him a second to catch on, and then he said, "No, not *rafters*. *Rapture*. That's when Jesus is coming back. All the Christians will leave the earth and join Him in the air. If you're not saved, you'll be in big trouble. It's called hell."

> I don't go to church. I don't like church, and I don't need church. I can sleep better in my bed.

I shook my head and smiled. "You know I can't go. I promised my mama I'd stay in school and get my degree. It doesn't matter who comes for me; I'm staying at Louisiana Tech." Then with a smug expression, I told him, "After that, I'll be glad to fly away with you."

FOOTBALL...AND MORE

I worked out all summer so I'd be in good shape for the next season of football. When I returned to campus, I made a point of stopping at Denny's room. He was there. I'd been waiting all summer to zing him: "So, you got left behind. I guess you're a sinner just like me!"

Denny smiled. He was glad to see me, but he couldn't miss the opening I'd unexpectedly given him. He grinned, "No, not *just* like you."

During our sophomore year Denny and I went at each other in good-natured banter. He said I was on this top ten list of most unlikely people to be saved, and I told him I was offended if I wasn't number one.

The next year the coach recruited a new quarterback named John Booty. I saw it as my civic duty to put him under my protective wing and warn him about Denny. On his first day I explained, "John, you'd better watch out. There's a guy on our team who's a religious fanatic. He actually enjoys Bible studies and church! Crazy, I know. He must be the most boring, irrelevant guy on earth. He's tried to convert me. Can you believe it? You'll be smart to stay away from him. His name is Denny."

John and Denny were both quarterbacks, so they spent a lot of time together. I noticed they seemed to enjoy each other, and they complimented each other on good passes in practice. It appeared that Denny was making inroads in John's mind. One day I walked past John's room, and I saw he had a Bible open on his desk. I blurted out, "What's that?" John was too gracious to state the obvious. He just smiled, so I asked, "Have you been talking to Denny?"

"Yes," he said calmly.

"What happened?"

"I got saved."

I was shocked. I couldn't believe he could be so dumb to believe what Denny was telling him. I turned and stormed out of the room. John started attending Denny's Bible studies, and they prayed together. I suspected they were praying for me! It was outrageous. All football season and that winter John and Denny talked, studied the Bible, and prayed.

During my junior year our team was outstanding. In fact, Louisiana Tech won the national championship for our division with a twelve and zero record. When spring break approached, I had big plans to go to Galveston, Texas, with about twenty other players for a blow-out week of parties. On Tuesday night before spring break started on Friday, I had a dream—but not an ordinary dream. I dreamed that I was stone drunk and driving my car in Galveston. I lost control of the car, flipped over, and slammed into a tree. The car caught on fire. Suddenly, in my dream, I stood in front of a gate. A man stood in front of me. I said, "Wow, this is heaven. Are you going to open the gate for me?"

The man asked, "Who are you?"

I answered, "I'm Glen Boom Boom Berteau."

He said, "I don't know you."

I asked him, "Do you know Denny Duron?"

The man replied, "I know him, but I don't know you."

I was shaken. "What do you mean you don't know me?"

The man explained, "I've been trying to talk to you, but you haven't listened."

"What are you talking about?" I insisted. "If you were talking, I'd have known about it."

He told me, "I was talking to you through Denny."

I was stunned, and then he said a single word that sent shudders down my spine: "Depart."

Instantly in my dream a trapdoor opened, and I fell from light into indescribable darkness. I couldn't see my hand in front of my face, but suddenly I felt intense, unbearable heat. My skin began to melt! At that moment

I awoke and sat straight up. I was sweating and breathing hard. My sheets, T-shirt, and hair were sopping wet. It took a few seconds to realize it had been a dream. It all seemed completely real. I turned on the light and ran to the mirror. My face was flushed and splotchy. It looked like it had been burned! For the first time in my life I realized: There's a real hell, and I'm going there!

Like many people (and you don't have to grow up in New Orleans to believe this) I thought hell was a huge party for bad, rowdy people—people like me. I envisioned it as a place where there aren't any rules, so you can do anything you want all the time—loud rock music, drugs, friends, and laughs. What's not to like? And heaven...I thought of heaven as the most awful, boring place imaginable: goofy people wearing robes playing harps and singing horrible songs off-key. From the dream I had a very different view of heaven and hell—well, hell, anyway. I realized hell is a huge barbecue, but I was going to be the one roasting on the spit!

You'd think the dream would be enough for me to go down the hall, barge into Denny's or John's room, and fall on my knees crying out to Jesus. It didn't happen. Like a lot of people who experience dramatic wake-up calls, I ignored the dream. I'm not alone. I've known people who were in near-fatal car accidents or faced life-threatening diseases, family breakups, financial collapse, and lots of other loud messages from God to get their attention, but they ignored Him. When I got up the next morning, it was like the dream never happened—at least, that's the way I wanted it to be. Actually, I had a nagging sense in the back of my mind that the earth had just tilted on its axis.

That was Tuesday night. On Wednesday before spring break John came by my room to invite me (for the zillionth time) to come to the Bible study he and Denny were holding that night. I'd turned them down so many times that I had my lines memorized. I snapped, "I'm not going to your boring Bible study. I don't know why you keep asking me. I haven't gone for three years. What makes you think I'm going to suddenly change my mind now?" I then said something that showed a deeper motive for my resistance. "And besides, I'm the leader of the sinners. People will laugh at me if I go with you. I have a reputation to maintain!"

This time, however, something was going on inside of me. I grabbed John and threatened to slug him. He was a quarterback, but I was a running back. I knew I could take him. He knew it too. For some reason my threats didn't intimidate him. He looked at me and said, "OK, Glen. I'll make a deal with you. If you come this one time, I'll never ask you again. That's my deal. What do you think?"

I thought about it a second and then told him, "Deal. I'll be there."

That night I made sure I didn't go into Denny's room on time. I wanted to be cool and walk in late. When I opened the door, I saw twenty-five guys from our team crowded in his room—and a bunch of them were going with me to Galveston in a couple of days! I tried to sneak in the back and hide, but Denny was too excited about me being there to ignore me. Every eye turned to look at me. Jaws dropped,

> I realized hell is a huge barbecue, but I was going to be the one roasting on the spit!

eyes widened, and more than a few mumbled something like, "Can you believe this? It's Boom Boom!"

Denny started preaching about Jesus being able to save people with the darkest souls and the most evil lives. He was pointing at me! Then he asked people to close their eyes so sinners could repent and be saved. Everybody bowed their heads and closed their eyes—everybody but me. I wasn't going to let Denny do anything crazy like hit me in the head. I didn't know how people got saved, but I wasn't going to take any chances. Denny asked people to raise their hands if they wanted to be saved. Out of the corner of my eye I saw a guy who was going with me to Galveston raise his hand. I was near him, so I whispered, "Put your hand down! Denny won't let you go with me to party at the beach if you get saved. Put your hand down quick!" Then another guy who was going with me put his hand up. Good grief; Denny was ruining all my plans!

At that moment I looked up. Denny was staring a hole right through me. He was waiting for the Holy Spirit to work in my heart and for me to raise my hand.

In an instant the pattern of my life became crystal clear. I'd devoted my entire life to drinking, playing music, and excelling on the football field. I had lots of friends and enjoyed a measure of acclaim. But suddenly I realized my life was a huge vacuum—completely empty. I'd been trying to fill the gaping void in my heart with all kinds of pleasures and prestige, but it hadn't worked.

Denny was waiting for me to raise my hand, but I didn't. He finished praying and then said the meeting was over. The guys filed out of the room, some laughing and talking, some quiet and reflective. I tried to look cool. I didn't want anybody to know what was going on inside me at that moment. I didn't have butterflies. They were more like attack helicopters! I walked to my room, opened the door, and walked in. When I turned to close it, Denny was standing in the doorway. I held up my hand and barked, "Look, just leave me alone! OK? Just leave me alone." But Denny didn't leave.

In the whirlwind of my mind and heart I was counting the cost of becoming a follower of Jesus Christ. I told Denny, "Look, I don't want to claim I've been born again and still live the same life of selfishness and sin. I've laughed at people who are hypocrites, and I don't want to become one of them. On the day I announce I've become a Christian, everybody on campus will be shocked. Do you understand that?" He just nodded. I kept on: "If I'm not honest and sincere, I'll be the butt of a million jokes. And besides, I don't like the idea of my friends calling me the same names I've been calling you and John for the last three years of college." Denny didn't flinch. I guess he was well aware of the things I'd been saying about him. I kept going in a torrent of words: "Then there's my family. What in the world will they say if I called to tell them I'd been born again? They'll think I've lost my mind!"

Denny could tell God was working in a powerful way. He just stood there smiling. Finally I took a deep breath and let it out. I told him, "But you know, I really don't want to go to hell." I'd been walking around the room, looking this way and that as I tried to talk myself out of trusting in Jesus, but now my eyes locked on Denny's. I told him, "Denny, be honest with me. Don't lie to me. Don't take me on a trip so I look like a fool. Tell me the truth. Is all you've been saying just crazy, silly stuff, or will

Jesus really save me? Will He really forgive me? Will He give me the joy you've been talking about all these years?"

He nodded, "Yes, that's exactly right. He will."

At that moment it felt like God took me by the back of my neck and dragged me down to the floor. I got on my knees. Denny almost shouted, "Boom Boom, you're going to do it! Pray, Boom Boom, pray!"

Pray? What would I say? I wasn't exactly skilled and experienced in the art of prayer. I created a blend of the Lord's Prayer: "Hail Mary, full of grace" and "Now I lay me down to sleep," but those didn't seem to fit. I looked up at Denny with an expression that asked for help. He said, "Just ask Jesus to forgive you and come into your life."

"That's it?" I asked.

"Yeah," he grinned. "That's plenty."

I prayed, "Lord, I confess my sins. Please forgive me and come into my life." At that moment in my dorm room at seven thirty-five on a Wednesday night before spring break, God took twenty-one years' worth of evil, selfishness, anger, pride, and fear off my shoulders. Some people don't feel much of anything when they turn to Christ, but I sure did. A flood of forgiveness, love, and peace overwhelmed me. As peace overwhelmed me, tears flowed down my face and puddled on the rug. Through my tears I said, "This is real!" Before that moment I thought Jesus was an historical figure like Robin Hood or Daniel Boone, or maybe a fictitious character like the Easter Bunny. Now I knew He was a real person I could know, love, and follow.

Some people struggle after they've made a decision to follow Jesus. They feel tempted to go back to their old way of life, and they doubt their salvation experience. That didn't happen to me. Jesus was so real that I've never been attracted to that old life since then. Suddenly everything changed. The attractions of drinking and partying now looked stupid and empty. The thirst for acclaim melted away because I had what I'd always hoped fame would give me: genuine love—not a counterfeit based on my performance, but authentic love based on God's amazing grace that can never be taken away.

TALK OF THE CAMPUS

In the days after spring break people were talking about me all over campus. "Did you hear Boom Boom Berteau got saved?" (I could take their amazement one of two ways: either I was so popular that whatever I did made news, or I was such a hardened, incorrigible sinner that no one could believe somebody like me could become a Christian. I'm pretty sure it's the second reason.) The news that I'd gotten saved caused a wave of God's power on the campus. Suddenly a lot of other people were finding Christ and getting saved.

A couple of weeks later reporters and photographers from *Sports Illustrated* came to campus to do a feature on our team. We'd won the national championship the year before, and we

> I thought Jesus was an historical figure like Robin Hood or Daniel Boone, or maybe a fictitious character like the Easter Bunny.

were ranked number one in the nation again in our division. We had a great team. A number of the guys they interviewed went on to have successful careers in the National Football League. They interviewed Denny, our quarterback, and me, the running back, as well as several other players on offense and defense. This process, though, had an odd twist. They had never had to schedule interviews with players who were coming from a baptismal service at a swimming pool! So many people were getting saved that Denny had us all go to the Tech Olympic pool. The magazine photographers took a picture of Denny baptizing me—very unusual and very cool.

One night I was in my room when Denny came by to see me. He looked at all the rock music posters and my guitar. He asked, "Why don't you play the song 'Amazing Grace'?"

I said, "Never heard of it. Is it a Hendrix song?"

At first Denny couldn't tell if I was serious or not. Finally he realized it was an honest question. He shook his head and laughed. "No, it's a song about God's love and forgiveness. Let me hum it for you." He hummed the tune. After he left the room, I picked up my guitar—the one often hooked up to amps so loud they'd blow paint off the walls—and I picked out the chords of the song.

A day or so later Denny walked by and heard me playing the tune. He poked his head in my door and said, "Hey, that's cool. You're pretty good." He paused for a second, and then it looked like he had a great idea. "We need a guitar player for our band. Are you interested?"

A band? Denny? I had no idea. I said, "What's the name of your band?"

He said, "The Vessels."

That sounded like the lamest name for a band in the history of the universe. He could tell I didn't understand, so he explained, "You know, vessels. We hold the flow of the Spirit. Do you want to join us? I think you'd fit in really well."

EVANGELIZING WITH THE VESSELS

In spite of the lame name, I joined Denny's band. We were as cool as all the other bands of that era: striped maroon pants, wide white belt, long hair, and crosses on chains around our necks. My first gig with them was at Denny's dad's church. Denny was going to preach, and his band was playing too. He told me it was a Pentecostal church, but I had no idea what that meant. He might as well have told me it was a church for Martians. He said I could bring my Bible, but he hadn't realized I didn't own one. I grew up a Catholic, and we didn't carry Bibles to church, read them at home, or own several versions for our personal study. We had rosary beads and cards with pictures of saints on them. Denny didn't ask me to bring any of those. That's good, because I didn't have any of them either. I couldn't have found Genesis if my life depended on it.

I brought my amplifier to the church. As we were setting up, I wheeled it down the aisle. An older lady looked at me and put her hands over her ears. I said, "Ma'am, what's wrong?"

She growled, "It's too loud, son! It's way too loud!"

I said, "Uh, ma'am, I haven't even plugged it in yet."

She wasn't convinced by my piercing logic. She told me bluntly, "But it's going to be too loud. Look how big it is! It's too big for this church."

I turned the volume down for her sake. We didn't practice. Denny just told me to listen, find the chords, and play along. Cool. I could do that. A few minutes later the service started. He came up and started singing. He sang two songs, one about the blood of Jesus and the other about the blood of the Lamb. I picked out the chords, but I wondered, "What in the world is this? A vampire cult? Why don't they sing cool songs and have a party? No wonder none of my friends go to these churches!" After the congregation sang a song or two, I thought, "Poor Jesus. He must have been bleeding all the time!"

After Denny preached, I was ready to go back to the dorm. The church service had been interesting but very confusing. Before he finished, though, he gave an invitation. He said, "I want to ask those of you who want to receive the baptism of the Holy Spirit to come forward. One of our people will pray with you." Several people came up to the front. Denny motioned to one of the singers in the band to pray with one of the people. Then he motioned to me to pray for another person. He whispered, "Boom Boom, will you pray for him?"

I wanted to shout, "Pray what? I've only prayed one prayer in my entire life. I have no idea what you want me to do!" I whispered, "Denny, cut me some slack here. All I have is a 'getting saved' prayer. I don't have a Holy Spirit prayer."

He came over and explained, "Just put your hand on the person and say, 'Lord, baptize him in the Holy Spirit in Jesus's name.' That's all you have to do. God will do the rest. Now, go!"

A young man knelt at the altar. His hands were shaking. I thought, "This guy doesn't need the Holy Spirit. He needs some Valium or Xanax or something. He's got the shakes. Maybe he's an addict and is going through withdrawals." I wanted to look for a doctor, but Denny nodded toward the guy and whispered again, "Boom Boom, go over and pray for him."

I walked over to the man and said, "Hey buddy, what do you want?" (Pretty sensitive, don't you think?)

He looked up and said, "I want the Holy Spirit!"

I said, "Cool; hang on just a minute."

I walked back over to Denny and said, "Uh, he wants that Holy Spirit thing."

Denny insisted, "Good. Pray like I told you a minute ago."

I had hoped Denny would take over for me, but that didn't work. Now I had to take matters into my own hands. I walked back over to the young man kneeling at the altar. I told him, "Look, bro, I'm going to pray for you to get the Holy Spirit. Are you cool with that?" He nodded. I felt like I needed to issue a disclaimer, so I explained, "Hey, I have no idea what's going to happen, but you look like you need some help. I'm going to put my hand on your head, so don't freak out. I know it's weird, but that's what Denny told me to do. OK?"

He nodded, so I prayed, "Lord, this guy wants the Holy Spirit. He wants it real bad, so in Jesus's name, there you go."

Immediately the man started speaking in tongues! I ran over to Denny, but this time I didn't whisper. "Hey, man, you gotta see this! I just touched him and prayed, and he instantly turned into a foreigner! Help me turn him back!"

Denny just laughed. He said, "Boom Boom, that's the Holy Spirit at work in this guy's life."

"Can't be," I insisted. "He doesn't make any sense."

Denny nodded to another person at the altar and said,

"Go over and pray for that lady. She needs the Holy Spirit too."

My method seemed to work the last time, so I stayed with it. I walked over to the lady and asked, "So, what do you want?"

She replied, "I want the Holy Spirit."

Cool. I knew the drill. I explained that I was going to put my hand on her head and pray for her. She seemed fine with that plan. I put my hand on her and asked the Holy Spirit to come in Jesus's name. *Bam!* She started speaking the same language the guy had been speaking. Well, I wasn't sure it was exactly the same, but they sure sounded a lot alike—which means I couldn't understand either one.

> He looked beneath my cocky façade and saw a person who desperately needed the love, forgiveness, and power of Jesus Christ.

I looked at my hand and thought, "I have a new talent. I can touch people and pray for them, and then they talk funny. I wonder if I need a license to carry a concealed hand."

While all this was going on, Denny was still preaching. He told the congregation, "The Holy Spirit is God's gift to us. He gives us the power to fight against the forces of the enemy, and He equips us to live the way God wants us to live. Every believer needs the Spirit's love and power."

People at the altar were crying tears of joy and relief. People in the seats were crying too. I tried to put it all together. I thought, "OK, this is good. When I got saved the other night, I experienced God, and now I see there's even more. I definitely want the Holy Spirit!"

I had no idea what to do because I didn't know church etiquette. While Denny was preaching, I walked over to him, grabbed his hand, and put it on my head. He leaned over and whispered, "Boom Boom, what are you doing?"

I said, "I want the Holy Spirit too. So do me."

Denny smiled and prayed for me, and I began speaking in tongues—right on the platform.

I could tell many more stories about those first few weeks as a new Christian. Everything was new to me, and Denny included me in everything he was doing for the Lord. He was an incredible friend. He's an example of what this book is about. He could have remained comfortable in his Christian world of church and Bible school, but he "left the building" to go to a state college so he could share and model the gospel of Jesus Christ. He never communicated that he was better than anyone else. He just loved everyone so much that he wanted them to experience the fabulous riches of Christ. Denny was a giver, not a taker. To Denny no one was beyond the love and power of God—even a hardened, selfish sinner like Boom Boom Berteau.

There are people like me in your company, on your street, in your city, and maybe living under your roof. It's easy to write those people off, especially after making an attempt or two to reach out to them. Denny didn't quit after a couple of attempts to reach into my heart. That guy simply wouldn't take no for an answer! He was never pushy, obnoxious, or condemning. He looked beneath my cocky façade and saw a person who desperately needed the love, forgiveness, and power of Jesus Christ.

My story isn't unique, and neither is Denny's. I've become Denny. After I met Christ, I had a lot of catching up to do, but I realized that the tough, hardened people—and the frightened, timid ones—we meet every day have empty hearts. If we love them enough, God may use us to crack open a door for His love to flood in. You have to admit that it's unmistakably beautiful.

At the end of each chapter I've included a few questions. Use these to stimulate your thinking, prayers, and conversations with family and friends. If you're in a class or small group using this book, these questions are your discussion guide.

THINK ABOUT IT...

1. What kinds of people want us to think they're beyond the love and grace of God? Why do they want us to see them this way?

2. What's your story? What did God do to get your attention? Did He use the persistent love of a friend or family member to soften your heart? What finally opened the door for you to experience God's grace?

3. Is there a Boom Boom Berteau in your life? Have you given up on that person? What would it take for you to have your hope rekindled that God might use you (or someone else) to touch that person's heart? Do you even believe it's possible? Why or why not?

two

THE GURU, THE SATANIST, THE HARE KRISHNA, AND THE GRASSHOPPER

THE GOSPELS TELL us that some people found Jesus repulsive, but many saw Him as incredibly attractive. The ones who flocked to Him weren't on the guest list for the best parties. They were the prostitutes, tax collectors, blind people, immigrants, lepers, and those who were demon possessed. Most of us have moved to communities to steer clear of "undesirables" like these, but Jesus delighted in them. And not surprisingly they loved hanging out with Him. Even in the nicest neighborhoods, if we open our eyes, we'll notice people with big problems—people who need us to step into their lives with the love of Christ.

When we find Jesus to be beautiful, we delight in His kindness and marvel at His awesome power. As we're overwhelmed with Him, we open our hearts and invite Him to change us from the inside out. He makes us beautiful, and we have a profound impact on the people around us. In fact, we shine like stars! Paul explained this phenomenon to the Christians in Philippi:

> Dear friends, you always followed my instructions when I was with you. And now that I am away, it is even more important. Work hard to show the results of your salvation, obeying God with deep reverence and fear. For God is working in you, giving you the desire and the power to do what pleases him. Do everything without complaining and arguing, so that no one can criticize you. Live clean, innocent lives as children of God, shining like bright lights in a world full of crooked and perverse people.
> —PHILIPPIANS 2:12–15

People are watching. They want to know if our faith is real, and they want to know if Jesus is as loving and wonderful as they've heard. Or is it all just a game? When they interact with Christians, are the people who claim to know Jesus just as angry, complaining, and cynical as everyone else?

If we think we can add Jesus to our lives and expect Him to give us what we want, we're treating Him like the appliance repairman. We invite Him into our lives when we need something fixed, but there's no relationship, no wonder, no love. In the same letter Paul said, "Everything else is worthless when compared with the infinite value of knowing Christ Jesus my Lord" (Phil. 3:8). What was he talking about? Fame, wealth, comfort, and pleasure—the things that most people long for and strive to get. But when compared to knowing Jesus, nothing else comes close. For that reason Paul compared himself to a drink offering poured out in gratitude to the Lord.

When we find Jesus to be beautiful, we pour ourselves out to Him and for Him—not because we ought to, but because we want to show our joy and gratitude for being His.

Paul could have been describing Denny Duron in his letter to the Philippians. I never heard Denny complain, and he was never cynical. He poured himself out in joy, thanks, and service because Jesus was the most precious thing in his life. As I watched him over the years we played football together, I saw an example of someone who shone brightly in a dark world—including my dark world. When I got saved, Denny's lifestyle was imprinted in my heart. I wanted to tell anyone who would listen about Jesus.

> If we think we can add Jesus to our lives and expect Him to give us what we want, we're treating Him like the appliance repairman.

After I got saved and joined Denny's band, I was fired up about Jesus! I was still trying to find my way around the Bible, but I was eager for God to use me. A church in Kansas City asked the band to come and play. We drove up and prepared for our gig. We had a free afternoon, so Denny said, "Let's go to the park and find some people we can tell about Jesus."

I'd seen Denny talk to football players and other people on campus, and I'd heard him preach at church, but this was new to me. I said, "Denny, that's cool and all, but I'm not sure what to do."

He said, "Just tell them what Jesus has done for you. That's all they need to hear."

I'd never gone through any evangelism training. I didn't know any techniques, and I didn't have any gospel booklets to give away. I just had my story. We drove over to the park and got out. I looked at the people sitting, walking, playing with dogs, chasing children, and relaxing in a dozen different ways. I had no idea who to talk to, so I walked over to a young man who was alone. With great tact I stated, "Hey, you don't know me, but I want to tell you what Jesus did in my life."

His eyes widened, and he responded, "Wait a second. Do you know what I'm doing tonight?"

I could think of about a hundred options, but I decided not to go through the catalog with him. I wondered if he had heard of our band, so I asked, "Are you coming to hear our band play tonight at the church?"

He looked at me like I had just landed from a distant planet. He shook his head. "No, no." Then he said, "You haven't heard? Guru Maharaji is going to be here tonight!"

The expression on my face must have communicated plenty. He repeated himself, but more slowly this time, like I was a three-year-old. "Guru Maharaji. Here. Tonight."

Somehow the look on my face must not have suggested enlightenment. He explained, "Don't you know? He's sixteen years old, and he's god!"

I'm from New Orleans, not Los Angeles or New Delhi, so I'd never heard of a guru. Since he mentioned God, I thought I'd go there. I asked, "So, do you really think he's God?"

The man was excited. "Oh, he's better than God!"

Now I was really confused. I mumbled, "How? Better than Jesus?"

He thought he had set the hook, and he was ready to reel me in. He tilted his head and smiled, "Oh, yeah. Why don't you come tonight to be enlightened? You'll see the glow around the stage and taste the nectar in the air!"

I was puzzled and replied, "I've never tasted nectar in the air."

He wasn't finished. He promised, "You'll be totally transformed. I guarantee it!"

I tried to be polite. I smiled as I shook my head and waved to him as I walked away. OK, that's my first witnessing experience. Were they all going to be this weird?

I walked for a few minutes to clear my mind, and then I felt I was ready to talk to someone else—someone who would be open to hear about Jesus. I saw a guy who looked completely normal. Nothing odd at all. I walked up to him and said, "Hey, I want to tell you what Jesus has done in my life." He looked puzzled, so I explained, "Our band is in town to play at a church. Why don't you come to hear us?"

"Can't come," he said curtly.

I wasn't sure how to respond. (No training, remember?) I shot back a witty reply: "I wish you could."

He explained, "Can't tonight. I'm going to a group that's studying the Satanic Bible."

"The what?"

"The Satanic Bible." He suddenly realized he needed to do some witnessing of his own, so he explained, "Before you swallow all that Jesus stuff, you need to read the Satanic Bible to see what's really true. It'll really help you out." He didn't try to convert me. After he made his pronouncement and gave his friendly advice, he just walked away. OK, that's number two.

The guy was confident and well read. A devil worshipper had more information about his unbelief than I had about my belief! I realized I needed to study to have more information so I could talk more intelligently to people. I knew I didn't have to argue them into faith, but I at least needed to be able to carry on a valid conversation and respond to their assertions about Jesus. I found Denny and said, "Man, I need to start reading the Bible. Can you help me?"

"Sure," he smiled.

The next week I flew to Los Angeles. During the whole flight I read passages in the Bible Denny gave me. When we landed and I walked into the terminal, I saw a group of people who looked like Indians wearing bathrobes. They had funny haircuts, played little cymbals and tambourines, and tried to stop people to talk with them. I leaned over to a man walking next to me and whispered, "What's up with them? Are they off the reservation?"

He looked at me to see if I was kidding. When he realized I was serious, he explained, "No, they're Hare Krishna."

One of them must have seen me looking at them. (Most people made a point of avoiding eye contact.) He jumped in front of me and asked, "Hey, friend, can I talk to you?"

Wait a minute. Isn't that my line? I asked, "What do you mean? Out of all the people getting off this plane, why do you want to talk to me?"

He smiled, "I want to give you something." He handed me a hardback book about Hare Krishna.

I took it and kept walking. "Thanks," I said over my shoulder.

He walked behind me and explained, "Some people give us money for the book."

"Oh, yeah. That's cool." I kept walking.

Now he was almost running to catch up with me. He insisted, "Sir, stop. Please stop! I need to get some money for the book. Please give me some money!"

I stopped and turned. "I thought you said it was a gift." He nodded and looked like he was going to launch into an hour-long explanation, so I told him, "Thanks for the gift." I turned and walked away as fast as I could walk without breaking into a sprint.

He wasn't finished. He ran after me and yelled, "Give me my book back! If you won't give me money, give it back!"

Everybody in the Los Angeles airport was watching this scene. I stopped and looked him in the eye: "Do you know what you can do with this book? Look, you're the one with a shaved head walking around here wearing a bathrobe. Does your mama know what you look like? You need to get a life! Here's what I'm doing with your book!" I walked over to a trash can and threw the book in it. I wasn't finished. I turned and growled, "The reason you came over to me is that I have something you need. You need Jesus, and you need a different book—the Bible. You need your life changed. Do you understand?"

He had probably taken a vow of nonviolence, but I think he wanted to hit me. All the people watching were aghast and amazed. I think some of them wanted to cheer, and some wanted to run away and hide. I'd handle the situation a bit differently today. I'd just been saved a few weeks, and the Spirit hadn't given me much kindness and wisdom at that point. Still, I didn't slug the guy. I saw that as evidence of the Spirit's work in me!

That night I was setting out materials at a church. I was alone in the lobby when a little guy walked in. He came up to me and almost whispered, "May I talk to you?"

This guy reminded me of the blind Shaolin monk on the television show *Kung Fu*. In the show the monk told Caine, the kung fu apprentice, "Do you hear the grasshopper at your feet?"

> No one ever told me they loved me before—not in my entire life.

The guy in the church lobby bowed and talked softly. I greeted him by saying, "Hello, grasshopper." I knew I'd blown it with the Hare Krishna. I'd been way too dramatic and drastic with him. This guy, though, seemed almost as strange, but I was determined to show him some love. I said, "Sure. Shoot. Ask away."

He reached over to a table and picked up a book. He waved it in front of himself and then looked at me. He asked, "What does God think of motion?"

I was sure I hadn't understood him. He was talking softly, and the question was absurd. Maybe he was asking a question about the Bible or directions to find a hamburger or something. I said, "Uh, come again?"

He spoke slowly (again, like I was a three-year-old). "What does God think of motion?" When he didn't get the quick-witted response he expected, he continued, "Like when I pick up this book and move it around?" He slowly moved the book around and then put it on the table again.

I thought back over all the things I'd heard preached in the last few weeks, and I even tried to remember physics classes in college. Nothing. I couldn't think of anything that remotely answered this guy's bizarre question. I shook my head and told him confidently, "God thinks motion is fine. He doesn't have a problem with it—none at all. If you want to pick the book up and move it, God says, 'All day. Have fun.' As far as God's concerned, motion is cool."

He looked puzzled, but he said softly, "Thank you." And he turned to walk out.

As he walked away, I said, "Hey, I just want you to know that I love you, and I'm praying for you. I'd love to see you in church."

He turned on a dime. "What did you say?"

I repeated, "Uh, I just said I'm praying for you and…"

"No," he interrupted. "Before that."

I had to think for a second, and then I remembered. "I said I love you."

He walked back toward me with his eyes wide open. "Why did you say that?"

Wow, the conversation just went from completely weird to intensely personal. I told him, "To be honest, I wouldn't have said that a month or two ago. In fact, I sure wouldn't have been in a church setting up for our band. And I didn't care about people—people like you. But I got saved. Jesus saved me, and now I care about people—especially people who are searching for God. Jesus found me, and He's changing me. He's put love in my heart for all kinds of people. It wasn't there before, so it has to be supernatural."

He looked at me as if I'd just escaped from an asylum, but I continued, "Jesus saved me, and He's changing me.

That's the truth. I'm not too sure about motion, but I'm completely sure about God's love."

He looked stunned. He said, "You said love from your heart, not your mind." After a few seconds he sighed, "No one ever told me they loved me before—not in my entire life."

I told him my story about resisting God and meeting Jesus in my dorm room a few weeks before. When I finished, I did what Denny did for me. I asked him if he wanted to pray to Jesus. He said he did, so right there in the lobby of that church the grasshopper got saved. He came to church to hear us play that night, and he'll never be the same. He had been studying all religions of the world, but now he began following the one true God.

SHARING THE WATER OF LIFE

Many of us in churches make two huge mistakes: we are preoccupied with worries and desires in our own lives, so we don't notice the needs of people around us, and we relegate our faith to an hour on Sunday (or an occasional Sunday). When I played football, our coaches talked to us a lot about holding the ball so we didn't fumble. Too many Christians fumble their opportunities to have an impact on others because they've taken their eyes off the ball. It's easy to do. The kids, the mortgage, the job, the bills, and the game seem so much more important than the unseen spiritual realities. If we stop and notice, though, we'll realize every person around us is crying out to God. We probably won't meet them in church. We interact with them at the grocery store, on the beach, at football games, at work, at the park, or in the mall. Many people appear to be apathetic or resistant, but if we peel down a layer or two, we find a genuine spiritual thirst. In fact, some of those who are crusty on the outside are marshmallows on the inside.

One time I was in Miami and grabbed a cab to go to the airport. As soon as I got in his car, the driver started cursing. It seemed that he was furious at everybody and everything. He hated his family, his country, and his taxi company. He hated preachers, immigrants, young people, and old people. It seemed that every other word spewing out of his mouth was a curse word. I tried to enter the conversation and say something positive, but he interrupted me. After the torrent subsided, I asked, "What do you dream of becoming? Do you plan to drive a taxi the rest of your life?"

I was shocked by his answer. He said softly, "No, I want to be a poet."

"An X-rated one?" I jabbed a bit.

He turned so I could see his smile. "No, I want to be creative. I want to write poetry that moves people's souls. I want my life to count."

"We all do," I agreed. I talked to him about the desire of every heart to be loved and to love. He'd been loud and angry, but now he was very quiet. When we arrived at my destination, I got out and asked him how much I owed him. I suddenly noticed tears running down his cheeks. He looked up at me and asked, "Would you tell me more before you get on the plane?" We talked a little

> Many people appear to be apathetic or resistant, but if we peel down a layer or two, we find a genuine spiritual thirst.

longer, and God opened his heart. We prayed together, and he got saved.

You don't have to have the gift of evangelism to care enough to look past people's apathy and resistance. If we aren't consumed with our own worries and demands, we'll find plenty of opportunities to enter meaningful—and sometimes life-changing—conversations with people every day.

I've learned to expect God to open doors at odd times and in the strangest places, but He still surprises me. One time my wife, Deborah, was shopping for clothes, and I went along to offer my expert advice on women's apparel. While she was trying something on, I talked to the owner of the boutique. I asked a couple of normal questions, but they led to places I hadn't expected. She poured out her heart to me that she and her two children were living with a man. She knew it was wrong, and she started crying. I prayed for her, and she got saved—right there between the belts and the underwear.

The love of God flows like a river. It's always in motion, unrestrained, and full of power to change the course of a person's life. Many of us, though, are more like stagnant ponds than mighty rivers. Through Jeremiah the Lord said, "For my people have done two evil things: They have abandoned me—the fountain of living water. And they have dug for themselves cracked cisterns that can hold no water at all!" (Jer. 2:13). For those who didn't grow up one hundred years ago on a farm, let me explain: A cistern was used to collect rainwater for household use. If you didn't live near a fresh, clear stream, you dug a cistern where water from rain was funneled for drinking, washing, and cooking. About twenty-seven centuries ago God said that

His people had stopped drinking from the flowing fountain of His love. Instead, they tried to get love and fulfillment through their own efforts. They dug a cistern, but it was broken and dry. That's tragic, but it's also stupid. Who would be so dumb to ignore a clear, cool flowing stream and end up dying of thirst looking at a dry pit? It just doesn't make sense, but that's what many Christians are doing today.

It's not like God's promises are unclear. In John's Gospel Jesus gave several metaphors and explanations of dynamic spiritual life. He told His disciples that being used to change lives was so fulfilling that He didn't even think about eating! He told them, "My nourishment comes from doing the will of God, who sent me, and from finishing his work" (John 4:34). At a huge feast people were involved in sacrifices and ceremonial washings. They thought those things would bring them joy and fulfillment. On the last day—the culmination of the feast—Jesus stood up, got everybody's attention, and shouted:

> "Anyone who is thirsty may come to me! Anyone who believes in me may come and drink! For the Scriptures declare, 'Rivers of living water will flow out from his heart.'" (When he said "living water," he was speaking of the Spirit, who would be given to everyone believing in him. But the Spirit had not yet been given, because Jesus had not yet entered into his glory.)
>
> —JOHN 7:37–39

On the night before He was arrested, Jesus explained spiritual life in terms the disciples could understand:

Yes, I am the vine; you are the branches. Those who remain in me, and I in them, will produce much fruit. For apart from me you can do nothing.... You didn't choose me. I chose you. I appointed you to go and produce lasting fruit, so that the Father will give you whatever you ask for, using my name.

—JOHN 15:5, 16

Do you feel like a dry, empty cistern, or is the love of Jesus flowing out of you into the lives of those you touch each day? Are your eyes on the wrong prize, or has pleasing God replaced self-absorbed pursuits? Have you tried really hard to measure up but never seem to make it? Recognize your desperate need for the love and power of God to delight your heart and transform your desires, attitude, and behavior. Do you see people around you as stepping-stones to get where you want to go—or maybe as hindrances? Look again. They're people God has put in your life, and He wants to use you to touch their hearts. Some of us think that ministry is only for pastors or those who are super spiritual. That's not true. All of us are masterpieces created by God to accomplish incredible things. Jesus assured us, "Do you think the work of harvesting will not begin until the summer ends four months from now? Look around you! Vast fields are ripening all around us, and are ready now for reaping" (John 4:35, TLB).

> In my experience people in our families, jobs, and neighborhoods are far more eager to hear the good news than the church is ready to share it.

EVANGELISM: OVERFLOW OF JESUS'S LOVE

When we become Christians, we get a new heart. It's no longer a heart of stone, but it's a heart that loves God and delights to join Him in the greatest adventure the world has ever known: transforming human hearts. We naturally want to honor the One who created us and bought us back from sin and death. We please Him with our love and loyalty. In our desire to honor Him, we also become aware of the things that bring Him sorrow. In my reading of the Gospels, I found eight things that displease Christ:

1. Fishing without catching (Luke 5:1–11)

2. Empty seats at the feast of God's salvation (Luke 14:15–24)

3. Sowing without reaping (Matt. 13:1–23)

4. A fig tree with no fruit (Mark 11:12–14)

5. Lost sheep (Luke 15:1–7)

6. Lost coins (Luke 15:8–10)

7. Lost sons (Luke 15:11–32)

8. Proclamations with no response (Mark 10:17–27)

Jesus told His disciples to "shake the dust off" their feet if people refused to accept them or their message (Luke 9:5, NIV). That's good advice, but today it's far more common that God's people don't share the message at all. In my experience people in our families, jobs, and neighborhoods are far more eager to hear the good news than the church is ready to share it.

People are waiting for us to open our mouths and talk to them about Jesus. We don't have to be eloquent, and we don't have to have all the answers. (By the way, I'm suspicious of anyone who doesn't occasionally say, "I don't know.") There are a few statements and questions I've used to break the ice and take a conversation a step further. They aren't a formula, and they aren't rigid. After all, Jesus communicated in very different ways with the people He met. For instance, His conversation with the woman at the well (in John 4) was the polar opposite of His confrontation with the demanding people who wanted Him to feed them again (in John 6). Look for obvious open doors, and ask pertinent questions about children, work, hobbies, sports, or anything else in the person's life. Begin by noticing what's important to them. Most people enjoy talking about their interests. Become an expert at asking great questions—not too probing and not too obvious...questions that are just right. After establishing rapport, I often ask, "Where do you go to church?" or "What can I pray about for you?"

Quite often people tell me where they're going to church. I never try to bait and switch! I always say, "That's fantastic! I hope you get a lot out of going there. Tell the pastor hello for me, and stay committed to the Lord."

Anybody can initiate a conversation that can lead to an eternal change of address. We can't wait for the paid professionals to do the work of leading people to Christ. A friend or family member wins about three out of every four new believers. Only one in a dozen or so is led to faith by a pastor. Jesus said, "The harvest is great, but the workers are so few. So pray to the Lord who is in charge of the harvest; ask him to send out more workers into his fields" (Matt. 9:37–38). We don't need more bosses in the harvest field; we need more workers. Jesus told us to pray that God will "send out more workers." The word for "send out" is the same one used for casting out demons. We expect God to use all of His divine power and authority to cast demons out of a person who is cruelly possessed. We need God to use the same power and authority to send His people into their neighborhoods, their kids' rooms, their trucks, offices, fields, and bleachers to share the most wonderful news ever announced.

> Anybody can initiate a conversation that can lead to an eternal change of address.

Some people read these words and have a tug in their hearts. They want to be open channels of God's Spirit flowing into the lives of those around them, but they feel a lot more like dry, broken pots. We need constant reminders that the gospel isn't *good advice* about cleaning up our act to make us acceptable to God; it's the *good news* of God's amazing grace to forgive, cleanse, and heal. In Peter's second letter he gives a list of godly traits (actually, a progression of spiritual growth). After it he explains:

> The more you grow like this, the more productive and useful you will be in your knowledge of our Lord Jesus Christ. But those who fail to develop in this way are shortsighted or blind, forgetting they have been cleansed from their old sins.
>
> —2 Peter 1:8–9

Did you get it? If we're not growing, it's because we've forgotten the glory and wonder of Christ's forgiveness! We don't ever "get beyond" grace. It's the beginning of our spiritual lives, it assures us every step of the way, and it motivates us to live for the One who gave Himself for us. That is what Peter is saying.

Who are the people God has put in your life? Are some of them as difficult as Boom Boom Berteau? Are they as weird as the guy following a guru, as scary as a Satan worshipper, as odd as a Hare Krishna, or as fragile as a grasshopper? Are they as angry and tough as a cursing taxi driver or as thin-skinned as a guilt-plagued mom? They are all our neighbors, and they are all hurting under the surface.

Oh, I know, you have excuses—really good excuses for keeping your heart closed and your mouth shut. You don't know the Bible well enough. Your story isn't as dramatic as some others. You don't have time to invest in that person. You have a bad habit you can't shake. Yeah, yeah. I've heard them all. They're all smoke screens and distractions. What if Jesus had used excuses? He could have complained, "Man, these people are so dense. And the cross—it's way too painful. No, I think I'll pass." He faced the darkest night of human history. He wanted to bail out, but He didn't. He chose to do the Father's will no matter what the cost. He was willing to die for us...so what does it mean for us to live for Him?

When people cut me, I bleed. When people cut us in conversations, what comes out? Is it the love of God spilling out of us because we're so full of Christ, or do we bleed anger, judgment, apathy, greed, fear, or pride? Let the love of Jesus fill you up so much that you overflow. That's what evangelism is—nothing less and nothing else.

THINK ABOUT IT . . .

1. Have you ever tried to tell somebody about Jesus? When did you feel confident about it? When were you confused or afraid as you took that step?

2. It's been said that success in witnessing is sharing the message of Christ in the power of the Holy Spirit and leaving the results to God. Why is this an important perspective? What happens when we think we have to manufacture the results?

3. Paraphrase these two verses:

For my people have done two evil things:
They have abandoned me—
    the fountain of living water.
And they have dug for themselves cracked
    cisterns
    that can hold no water at all!
—JEREMIAH 2:13

"Anyone who is thirsty may come to me! Anyone who believes in me may come and drink! For the Scriptures declare, 'Rivers of living water will flow out from his heart.'" (When he said "living water," he was speaking of the Spirit, who would be given to everyone believing in him. But the Spirit had not yet been given, because Jesus had not yet entered into his glory.)
—JOHN 7:37–39

4. What are some ways to begin a casual conversation with people? How can you tell what interests them? What are a couple of good questions to turn the conversation to Christ?

5. When you're cut, what comes out? How can reminders of Jesus's love and forgiveness change what comes out?

three

THE RING AND THE ALTAR

FROM PERSONAL EXPERIENCE I know that the moment a woman receives an engagement ring is a supreme highlight of her life. I've only been there for one of these occasions, but I can imagine that every woman is as thrilled as Deborah was when I gave her a ring. People who aren't married don't have to think too hard to connect with this emotion. Movies, family stories, and ads for jewelry stores focus on that powerful, precious, and pivotal moment in a woman's life.

A ring doesn't mean the person is married, but it's the symbol that a strong commitment is right around the corner. In giving it, a man is saying, "You belong to me, and I belong to you." It's a promise before the promise, a commitment before the commitment, a vow before the vow. When I gave a ring to Deborah, it was tangible evidence of my pledge and love. Before we married, it was a promise of our future. After we married, it has been a reminder of our joyful, solemn covenant to belong to each other.

Deborah's ring is far more valuable than the metal and stone in it. Women don't respond to losing an engagement ring like misplacing their car keys. When a woman loses her engagement ring, it's catastrophic! Adrenaline rushes through her body, and she goes into panic mode! She searches everywhere until she finds it. Why is the engagement ring so valuable? Because it represents the treasure of loving and being loved, of having the security she longs for and desperately needs.

I have lots of pictures of Deborah. In many of them her hands—and her ring—can be clearly seen. I keep my favorite pictures in my office. It's not that halfway through a day I hit myself in the head and think, "Gosh, I can't remember what my wife looks like. What's her name?" No, it's not like that at all. I love to look at her smiling face all hours of the day. Her love is an anchor to my soul. We're partners, friends, and lovers. I look at her pictures as reminders that God has given me the very best. (No offense to other women, but that's the way I feel.)

John says in Revelation that the church of all believers is "the bride of Christ" (Rev. 19:7–9; 21:2), and the concept is implied in many other passages. There are, of course, many metaphors God uses to describe His relationship with us: vine and branches, shepherd and sheep, father and children, builder and building, master and servants, king and His people, head and parts of the body, and husband and bride. (Some men may object to being called "the bride of Christ," but women are included as "sons of God." If you bristle at these descriptions, get over it. Be thrilled you're included!)

In the next chapter we'll explore the concept of being a beautiful bride. For now, though, we want to look at the glorious anticipation and promise of the ring and walking to the altar to become one with Christ.

The ring, as we've seen, is a promise of a future commitment. When a couple goes to the altar to marry, they make vows and enter a covenant relationship. In the Old Testament the altar was the focal point of the temple. It was where sacrifices were made and vows were spoken. Some church traditions don't have altars any more because they believe the ultimate sacrifice has already been made. That's exactly right, but altars are also meant for vows, so they still have great significance. When a couple comes to the altar of the church, they're standing on holy ground. From ancient times God consecrated the altar for moments of commitment. The couple may have other things on their minds at that moment, but a good pastor will have explained the rich spiritual meaning of the place where they will speak their vows to one another.

God relates to people through covenants—agreements between God and human beings, conditional or unconditional. In the pages of the Bible we find God's covenant with Adam and Eve, Noah, Abraham, Moses, and David. But throughout those years another covenant was coming. Through Ezekiel God promised, "And I will give you a new heart, and I will put a new spirit in you. I will take out your stony, stubborn heart and give you a tender, responsive heart. And I will put my Spirit in you so you will follow my decrees and be careful to obey my regulations" (Ezek. 36:26–27). A few hundred years later Jesus had dinner with His disciples to celebrate Passover. He broke the bread and poured the wine. He explained to them that from the next day, nothing would ever be the same. God was fulfilling His promise through Ezekiel to create a new heart. He was instituting a new covenant. Jesus raised the cup of wine and said, "This is my blood, which confirms the covenant between God and his people. It is poured out as a sacrifice for many" (Mark 14:24).

Covenants are crucial. When they're broken, it's not like breaking a fingernail. Covenant breaking is a tragedy, and it requires repentance, forgiveness, and restoration. For centuries God's people had broken their covenant with God. They couldn't live up to the laws, precepts, and rules He had prescribed, so He provided a new and better covenant: the sacrifice of Christ to cleanse us, make us whole, and transform our hearts.

Covenants—between God and man and between a man and a woman—define relationships, provide stability and security, foster intimacy, stimulate creativity, and allow people to flourish. Without this commitment people always wonder if they've done enough to keep the other person pleased, and they worry the other person will walk away. Covenants are the foundation of strong relationships. They aren't just words or meaningless symbols. They're the rock on which relationships are built.

Vows describe the nature of the covenant. In the Bible God made this pronouncement: "I will be your God, and you will be my people" (Lev. 26:12). That's covenant language that binds God to us and us to Him. The most significant covenant in human relationships is marriage. The vows we take describe the bond we're making. The man and woman are committing themselves to each other no matter what may come. The language may vary, but the words often say, "...to have and to hold from this day forward, for better or for worse, for richer or for poorer, in sickness and in health, to love and to cherish, as long as we both shall live."

In our day many people take covenants lightly. They say

they're Christians, but they value clothes, vacations, money, friends, television, or countless other things more than Jesus. You may ask, "Pastor Glen, how can you make that statement? You don't know them." Jesus said, "Wherever your treasure is, there the desires of your heart will also be" (Matt. 6:21).

How do we treat something or someone we treasure? We need to look no further than a couple in love. They delight in each other, and they demonstrate the value they put on each other by their constant thoughts about the person they love, the time they invest in finding the right presents and creating perfect moments, and the daydreams about the future. They invest all kinds of resources and time in saying, "I love you!" No one has to give them rules to follow to force them to demonstrate their affection. It flows out of them!

> Covenants are crucial. When they're broken, it's not like breaking a fingernail.

If we love God, we treasure Him, and we gladly invest everything into our relationship with Him. We marvel at the beauty of His love, wisdom, and strength, and we realize we'll never fully grasp the wonder of His greatness. In our love for Him God transforms us, and we become beautiful.

THE BEAUTY OF THE BRIDE

There has never been an ugly bride. Never. Women anticipate that day and devote countless hours (and their dad's money) to make themselves look gorgeous. I'll have to admit that I'm not an expert at this, but I've heard that women spend months dieting so they'll look great on their wedding day. They search until they find just the right dress so they'll have the perfect look. As the day approaches, they carefully plan with their maid of honor and bridesmaids. They may start early in the morning to have their hair done and their makeup just right. (I have no idea why it takes so long, but as long as I don't have to be part of it, I'm OK with the process.)

When the doors open and the bride takes her father's arm to walk down the aisle, every eye is on her. In all my years of doing weddings, I've never had a bride walk halfway down the aisle and turn around because she forgot to put on her makeup or her hair was still in rollers. No, she has prepared every detail so the moment will be unforgettable. She wants the man of her dreams to see her at her very best. And she's radiant!

As she walks toward the altar, her grinning fiancé is thrilled beyond words. He has waited for this moment, and he's ready to make a lifetime commitment to the woman walking toward him. Both of them may have dated dozens of people in the past, but no longer. They are making a vow—"before God and these witnesses"—to belong exclusively and completely to one another.

> The vows we take describe the bond we're making.

What does this moment have to do with God making us beautiful so that our fame spreads throughout the land in effective outreach? Everything. If we think we've joined a civic club where people have a common interest, we'll stick around as long as it makes us feel good. But we'll bolt as soon as we feel the least bit bored or inconvenienced. But marriage isn't like that. It's a permanent covenant—a binding, strong, and vibrant commitment through thick and thin. It is the foundation of our society. In the same way, our "marriage" with God as His bride is a permanent covenant. When we say "I do" to God, He says "I do" to us. We're beautiful on the day we go to the altar to begin our relationship with Him, and we become even more beautiful as we bask in the continual warmth of His love, kindness, wisdom, and strength. He's a wonderful fiancé who invites us to be His partner forever, and He's a magnificent husband who has proven His love by His ultimate sacrifice of life and blood. We can't ask for anything more.

Many couples spend thousands of dollars on wedding pictures, and they look at those photos again and again throughout their married lives. The rings on their fingers and the pictures are constant reminders of the covenant they made at the altar. But hearts drift, people become distracted, and the worries of life can crowd out the affection they enjoyed. The memories of being thrilled with each other's touch and voice can fade. A continual investment must be made into keeping the relationship vibrant, creative, and strong.

In the same way, a wonderful start to a relationship with God can become stale. Our zeal can fade and our love can grow cold. It can happen to an individual, and it can happen to a church. Jesus warned the church in Ephesus, "But I have this complaint against you. You don't love me or each other as you did at first! Look how far you have fallen! Turn back to me and do the works you did at first" (Rev. 2:4–5).

How can we tell if we've forgotten our first love? Here are a few signs:

- We get more excited about a new outfit, game, or fishing trip than we do about experiencing God's love.

- We think about God only on Sunday morning. Even then we sing halfheartedly, and our minds wander during the sermon.

- We seldom pray, and when we do, it's a grocery list of things we want from God. We don't spend time marveling at Him.

- We excuse our piddling sins and insist, "They're not that bad; besides, they don't really hurt anybody."

- We feel bored by stories of God's work in people's lives.

- We feel a nagging sense of guilt that things aren't right between us and God, but we don't do anything about it. Guilt becomes the new normal.

- We now see God's commands as limitations on our happiness.

- We delight in finding fault with other Christians who are so "stupid" or "legalistic" or "weird."

- We care more about others' approval than God's "Well done, good and faithful servant."

- We hear stories about people who are hurting, and we assume, "That's too bad, but it's not my problem."

- We feel energized by the bitterness we feel over an offense, and we refuse to forgive.

- We resent "being forced" to give our money to the Lord's work.

- We see God and His work as optional instead of central to our lives.

NEVER LOSE YOUR FIRST LOVE

Remember the old Righteous Brothers' song "You've Lost That Loving Feeling"? What can bring it back? Jesus was telling the church at Ephesus, "Don't you remember what it was like when you got saved? Think! Look at the wedding pictures! Feel the ring on your hand!" And He's saying the same thing to many Christians today:

- Remember how you felt when you got saved!

- Remember how excited people were when you told them you'd found Christ!

- Remember the fear and joy of learning to pray!

- Remember reading the Bible those first few months when everything was brand-new!

- Remember the sense of awe when you realized Jesus is Lamb and Lion, Savior and King!

- Remember what it was like to tell your story to unbelievers for the first time!

- Remember finding passages of Scripture that seemed like God was talking directly to you!

Many of us today are preoccupied with "the worries of this life, the lure of wealth, and the desire for other things" (Mark 4:19). Our hearts are primarily invested in things or people instead of in Jesus. We're grasping for more, we're worried we won't get as much as someone else, and we're afraid God won't come through for us.

Jesus was saying to the Ephesians, and He's saying to many people today, "You've lost your first love. You've drifted. I'm still here, still faithful, still in love with you, but your attention is on something or someone else. Come back to Me. I welcome you with open arms. I love you. Come back." God wants us to remember the covenant. We belong to Him, and He belongs to us. He's invisible, but we see His hand at work in all of creation and by the Spirit's work all around us. We may assume that our Husband has gone on a long trip and forgotten about us, but He hasn't. He's right here right now. When God's people complained that God had abandoned them, He compared His love for them with the tender and constant attention of a mother:

> If we want a God who always does what we want Him to do, we don't have a real God; we have a butler or a waiter.

Can a mother forget her nursing child?
　　Can she feel no love for the child she has
　　　　borne?
But even if that were possible,
　　I would not forget you!
See, I have written your name on the palms of
　　my hands.
　　　　　　　　　　　　　　—ISAIAH 49:15–16

Many people have a misconception of the Christian life. They joined up because they assumed God would make their lives better and more pleasant in every way. They came for the benefits. There are, for sure, plenty of benefits, but a covenant relationship isn't based on flimsy notions of superficial happiness. We're in…all in—for better or worse, in sickness and health, rich or poor. The deeper blessing is the hope—the rock-hard assurance—of God's love and purposes no matter what's going on in our lives. We live in the most affluent society the world has ever known. Most "poor" people in our country have more conveniences and technology than rich people a couple of generations ago. But instead of being thankful and generous, we've become soft, unrealistic, and filled with the poison of entitlement. When things don't go our way, we get upset with God and accuse Him of letting us down.

If we want a God who always does what we want Him to do, we don't have a real God; we have a butler or a waiter. If we want a God who always agrees with us and never challenges our perceptions, we don't have a real God; we have a Stepford God. (You may remember the book and movie *The Stepford Wives*, where men created robotic women who always said, "Yes, dear," and did whatever the men wanted.) Jesus didn't come to be our waiter. We needed much more than that. We needed a Savior who was also a King. He isn't our maid; He's our master, sovereign, and husband. The more we know Him, the more we're amazed at Him.

COMMITMENT TO PERMANENCE

Some of us have a camping mentality in our relationship with God. When I was younger, I often went camping. I might hike in the mountains or find a nice campsite in a national park and put up my tent for the night. Camping is fun and exciting. We feel the rush of being outdoors. There's the joy of sitting next to a campfire and making s'mores after dinner. And you never know what kind of critter is going to visit in the night. It's a lot of fun to go camping, but there's no long-term commitment. When we camp, we know it's temporary. We take just enough supplies to make it for a night or a few days. We're not going to live there but a day or two, so we don't invest much in the place. We're not going to raise a family in a tent, and if a storm gets too fierce, we drive back into town to find a hotel room for the night.

When Christians have a camping mentality, they are initially excited and enjoy the thrill, but they don't have a sense of permanence. They're there to be entertained. They might enjoy roughing it for a short time, but they fold up their tents and leave if the storms get too rough.

> The more we know Him, the more we're amazed at Him.

A covenant relationship isn't camping. It's a commitment to permanence. That's God's perspective of us, and it's our perspective of our relationship with Him. No matter what happens, God still rules. No matter how fierce the storm blows, God still cares. God is still on His throne. We have a covenant relationship—a marriage—with God. We need to remember that we've said "I do" to Him. And we need to constantly say to Him, "Jesus, You paid the price for me. You love me, and You bought me back from sin, death, and hell. I'm Yours—with no strings attached. Use me. Mold me. Lead me. There's nothing inside me that You can't use for Your glory, and there's nothing outside me that You can't turn into blessing—if I'll only trust Your wisdom, love, and power. You deserve all I have, and that's what I'm giving You."

What gives us this deep, strong, permanent sense of commitment to God? Some people try to live on rules. They use God's commands as a measuring stick to see if they're acceptable. When they believe they're doing well (or at least better than the people around them), they're filled with pride. When they realize they've blown it over and over again, they suffer nagging guilt. Those are the only two outcomes of trying to live by rules.

The other way to try to make life work is to throw off all the rules. "Hey, God is love, isn't He?" some people assert. "Surely He looks the other way when I sin." These people are self-indulgent and use people instead of loving them. They make a wreck of things for everybody, but they feel completely justified in their self-absorption.

There's another way. It's not a blend or balance of the other two. It's completely different. It acknowledges the rightness of God's rules and admits that we can't measure up to God's standard of holiness. Instead of causing us to feel arrogance or shame, it turns to Jesus's death on the cross as the perfect sacrifice—the perfect display of God's justice to condemn sin and His perfect love for sinners. Paul spent eleven chapters describing the wonders of God's mercy, grace, and love. Then he encouraged his readers (including us) to let the grace of God make a difference in how they live. He wrote:

> And so, dear brothers and sisters, I plead with you to give your bodies to God because of all he

has done for you. Let them be a living and holy sacrifice—the kind he will find acceptable. This is truly the way to worship him. Don't copy the behavior and customs of this world, but let God transform you into a new person by changing the way you think. Then you will learn to know God's will for you, which is good and pleasing and perfect.

—ROMANS 12:1–2

Did you get that? In response to Jesus's sacrifice of His life on the altar of the cross, we're filled with the wonder of His love, and we gladly offer ourselves to Him. Our bodies become an altar of grateful obedience and praise. Our lives become holy sacrifices poured out to please and honor Him. It's *the only reasonable response* to the kind of love Paul has taken such pains to describe for eleven chapters! When the Spirit works to transform our hearts, our "ought tos" become "want tos"—not immediately and not completely, but the transformation is very real. We don't give a few little things to God and give them grudgingly. We open our whole hearts to Him and give Him everything we have—just as a beloved bride gives herself to her husband on their wedding night.

Do you think this language is too dramatic and unseemly? It's not. Physical intimacy is common and easy, but emotional intimacy in any relationship is based on the strength of the commitment. In a marriage or a covenant relationship with God, we're totally secure, so we can be fully intimate. When we feel secure in God's love, we bring our broken lives to Him so He can touch us and heal us. We bring our hopes and dreams, as well as our fears and doubts. We're honest about our emptiness, and we invite Him to fill us. We tell Him about our confusion and trust Him to give us wisdom. We complain that things are taking too long, and He assures us that He hasn't forgotten. He tells us He knows, He cares, and He will provide at the right time. In this trusting relationship we realize we would have asked for what He has provided if we had known what He knew all along.

The Book of Psalms is God's hymnbook, but the psalms aren't normal songs. About half of them are expressions of anger, hurt, confusion, and disappointment. Shockingly, a few of them are cries for revenge! Why did God allow all of that in the Bible? Because He delights for His people to be secure enough to be honest with Him. He's not threatened by our anger, fear, or doubts. He invites us to wrestle with Him. In the interactions in these psalms virtually all of the painful emotions find resolution. We don't know how long it took, but the writers found God to be ultimately trustworthy.

Are you wearing a ring of promise from God? Have you come to the altar as a beautiful bride? Have you spoken the vow of the covenant with Him? Many people in churches are trying to live by the rules, but they haven't opened their hearts to Jesus. They've seen countless others meet Him at the altar, but they think being in the building and checking off the rules is enough. They haven't tasted the joy of a loving, covenant relationship with Him.

Some are wondering why they feel so distant from God. They know the right words to say and the songs to sing, but their hearts aren't moved by His love. Oh, they sense something from time to time, but their souls haven't been captured and enthralled by Jesus.

Others feel that God has let them down. They had

dreams, but those dreams have been shattered. Like the psalmists, they pour out their complaints that God hasn't come through to rescue their kids, change their spouse, give them a meaningful job, or heal their bodies. But unlike the psalmists, they haven't found resolution. The knife of hurt and disappointment is still stuck in their hearts.

Still others wrestle with destructive habits and consuming sins they can't shake. They struggle with addictions to drugs, alcohol, sex, food, gambling, work, shopping, fixing messed-up people, and self-pity. Yes, self-pity can be just as addictive as a drug. They've tried a million times to quit, but they don't have the power—and to be honest, they don't have the will to quit.

We can't be intimate with Jesus until we've entered the marriage. We won't have a changed heart until we've allowed Him to meet us at the deepest place of our souls. Without Him we're radically insecure. We jockey for position, we blame people for our mistakes, we hide our flaws, and we brag about our accomplishments. None of that fills our hearts in the least. Only Jesus changes us from the inside out.

Bring Him your fear, rejection, depression, rage, failure, arrogance, apathy, and self-pity. He already knows about it all. There's no need to hide anything from Him. He's not surprised, and He's not turning His back on you. Invite Him to overwhelm you with His love and power again.

If you went to the altar years ago but have drifted, feel the ring and look at the wedding pictures. Remember what it was like to be gloriously saved. Let your love be refreshed. You don't have to worry if Jesus will welcome you back. He's been waiting all this time for you to turn around and embrace Him.

Some people feel uncomfortable with this kind of language about our relationship with Jesus. They prefer to keep Him at arm's length. If they bring up the topic of church or God at all, they talk about theology or church strategy or administrative issues. Those things are important...in their place. But they aren't *ultimately* important. The Bible uses many metaphors to illustrate our connection with God, but the one that is most profound is marriage. We are the bride of Christ, the intimate ally of the sovereign King, the Savior's thrilled lover.

Many years ago Isaac Watts wrote a beautiful song titled "When I Survey the Wondrous Cross." The first and last stanzas capture the wonder and joy of experiencing Jesus's love.

> When I survey the wondrous cross
> On which the Prince of glory died,
> My richest gain I count but loss,
> And pour contempt on all my pride.
>
> Were the whole realm of nature mine,
> That were a present far too small;
> Love so amazing, so divine,
> Demands my soul, my life, my all.[1]

Yeah, I know. Some of the men reading this feel really awkward and are trying to laugh it off. Don't. You've been the strong initiator all your life, but not in this relationship. Jesus is the husband. He takes the lead, and you respond with affection and joyful obedience.

And some of the women reading this feel just as

uncomfortable, but for the opposite reason. They've been hoping a man would initiate love and protection, but they've been deeply disappointed. Now they aren't sure they can ever trust a man again—even Jesus.

Take the risk. Lower

> Without Jesus we're
> radically insecure.

your guard. Jesus has given you a ring of promise, and He's invited you to come to the altar to make a covenant of love with Him. Take Him up on it. He's never broken a promise, and He's not going to now.

THINK ABOUT IT...

1. What's the most wonderful, glorious, beautiful wedding you've ever attended? What made it so special?

2. What is a covenant? How is our relationship with God like the covenant of marriage?

3. What are some emotional and relational implications of us being "the bride of Christ"? Do you feel comfortable with talking about intimacy with Jesus? Why or why not?

4. Have you come to the altar? How does it affect you to realize Jesus sees you as a beautiful bride? (Men, be strong! Answer the question.)

5. In what ways does love so amazing, so divine, demand your soul, your life, your all?

four

THE BRIDE OF CHRIST

I'VE BEEN TO a lot of wonderful wedding receptions. After the ceremony the wedding party stays in the church to take pictures as the crowd files into the room or drives to the site where the reception is being held. As they wait, they might nibble on appetizers and grab something to drink. Before too long someone announces the members of the wedding party coming into the room, and finally (drum roll, please), the new couple walks through the doors beaming like a boy who got his first bike at Christmas! Everybody's smiling and applauding (except the bride's dad, who's still trying to figure out how much all this costs). The reception may be simple or lavish, a few trays of finger foods or an elaborate banquet dinner and a live band. It doesn't matter because every reception is a glorious celebration. It's a party of joy about where the couple has come from, the monumental event of the day, and a send-off into a life of love.

The Bible says that a day is coming that makes the most elaborate wedding reception today look like cold pizza and flat soda pop. In the Jewish culture weddings didn't happen in an hour or two. The feast and celebration often lasted up to a week! It was the biggest event of the season. In Revelation John tells us about the biggest blowout of all. In fact, the noise of the shouting and music was deafening to John. He wrote:

> Then I heard again what sounded like the shout
> of a vast crowd or the roar of mighty ocean waves
> or the crash of loud thunder:
>
> "Praise the LORD!
>   For the Lord our God, the Almighty, reigns.
> Let us be glad and rejoice,
>   and let us give honor to him.
> For the time has come for the wedding feast of
>   the Lamb,
>   and his bride has prepared herself.
> She has been given the finest of pure white linen
>   to wear."
>   For the fine linen represents the good deeds of
>   God's holy people.
>   —REVELATION 19:6–8

Centuries earlier God gave another prophet a vision of this event. Isaiah described the party this way:

> In Jerusalem, the LORD of Heaven's Armies
>   will spread a wonderful feast
>   for all the people of the world.
> It will be a delicious banquet
>   with clear, well-aged wine and choice meat.
> There he will remove the cloud of gloom,
>   the shadow of death that hangs over the
>   earth.
> He will swallow up death forever!

The Sovereign L ORD will wipe away all tears.
He will remove forever all insults and mockery
 against his land and people.
The L ORD has spoken!
In that day the people will proclaim,
"This is our God!
 We trusted in him, and he saved us.
This is the L ORD , in whom we trusted.
 Let us rejoice in the salvation he brings!"
      —I SAIAH 25:6–9

Who will be at this gig? All of those who have trusted in Jesus—people from every tribe, tongue, people, and nation. As John watched the vision of the wedding blast, an angel told him, "Blessed are those who are invited to the wedding feast of the Lamb" (Rev. 19:9). If you're thirsty, come to the fountain of living water. If you're hungry, feast on the bread of life. If you're lost, the Good Shepherd will find you. If you're broken and stained, say yes to the invitation of the healer and Savior.

In all weddings the bride is prepared, qualified, and gloriously revealed at the right moment. Today the bride of Christ is being prepared. We are qualified only because Jesus has paid the price for us and given us His righteousness and beauty. And someday we'll be revealed in all our glory. On that day we'll be part of the biggest party the world has ever known. How will we feel when we arrive at the party? Take the most meaningful worship, the greatest joy, the warmest love, and the most wonderful relief you've ever experienced, fold them together, and multiply it times one hundred. That's still not close to the sheer delight we'll experience on that day, but you get the idea.

It's hard to get our heads around John's vision of this future event. Some of us cringe when we think about our own weddings, and a few single people who attend a lot of weddings have made a mental checklist of all things to avoid when they eventually find the right person. I'm not sure I officiated at the craziest wedding and reception in the history of mankind, but it was in the top ten. When Deborah and I lived in Baton Rouge, Louisiana, one of our church leaders asked me to perform his wedding. He was marrying a girl who lived in Florida. Years earlier I was his youth pastor in Florida. I got directions to the church and drove east on Interstate 10. Near the place where the state takes a sharp turn toward Cuba, the directions said to turn left, which is north. I knew plenty of cities and resorts south of there, but the map didn't show much of anything north of the highway. I drove on a country road for a long, long way. I passed miles of pine forests and a few cattle ranches, but I didn't see many people at all. I had a few fleeting thoughts that I had entered "the Twilight Zone." Several times I wondered if I'd gotten the wrong directions.

I followed the directions and turned on a couple of other roads. Finally I saw a little church out in the middle of nowhere. My friend greeted me and introduced me to the groomsmen and his dad. We walked inside, and it looked like a greenhouse had exploded! Around the pulpit and the altar were dozens (maybe hundreds) of huge potted plants. It was an impenetrable jungle! I wanted to ask for a machete to hack out a spot where I could stand more comfortably, but I decided to try to make it work amid the greenery. I stood in the front with the groom and his guys. A couple of people in the wedding party solemnly walked up to light the candles, and then they walked back and sat down. In a few seconds I smelled something. I looked over, and the candles had caught some of the plants on fire!

My friend looked at me. The groomsmen looked at me. The people in the front row—the family members—looked at me. They all wanted me to do something about the fire...as if I'd come to a wedding with a fire extinguisher in my pocket! Some quick-thinking guy in the back ran to get a bucket of water and doused the flames. The hissing and smoke gave the room a particular smell and feel. It would have been fine for a campout, but not for a wedding. I asked everybody to sit down. I assured them everything was under control. Wrong.

The lady playing the organ on my left began to play, the doors in the back opened, and the bride and her father appeared in the doorway. She looked beautiful. She was so happy that she had a tear in her eyes. (She had no idea we'd just saved the building from being incinerated.)

The lady playing the organ was also the pianist for the event. The piano was on the other side of the church. When she finished playing for the bride to walk down the aisle, she didn't want to interrupt or call attention to herself, so she ran out the back door and came in the side door near the piano. She played a song, and then she ran out the side door and appeared a few seconds later at the other door. She ran to the organ and sat down. Did I mention that Florida is in the tropics? By the time she sat down the second time, she was sweating like an NFL linebacker. Her hair was a mess, and she looked like she had just wrestled a steer. I hoped nobody but me had noticed, but every eye was on her.

I tried to keep my concentration on the task at hand. I led the couple through the ceremony to the vows. I asked the groom to repeat them after me. When I said, "As long as you both shall live," he said, "Both as we long shall be."

That was it. I tried as hard as I could to keep a straight face, but I simply couldn't do it. I cracked up! The groom realized what he had said. He whispered, "Man, I'm nervous. Can't we move on?"

I introduced the Communion part of the ceremony. I explained the significance of the moment as the organist-sprinter darted out one door and in through the other to play the piano. I looked for the plate of the bread and the cup of juice, but I couldn't find it in all the bushes. As the piano played, I acted like Dr. Livingstone searching the jungles of Africa as I hunted for the elements. Finally I found the plate, but it was empty. No bread, no juice. I looked around to see if anybody could take a nonverbal cue and find these for me. At that moment I heard some rustling in the bushes. I moved some branches aside, and I saw a guy crawling behind the brush. I whispered, "Where's the juice and bread?"

He grimaced and mouthed, "There's not any. You'll have to fake it."

Fake it? How do you fake Communion? I turned around holding a plate that held no bread and a cup without any juice. I looked at the groom with an expression that said, "Hey, I'm doing the best I can. Just follow my lead." He grimaced and nodded. I didn't know if his bride got the message, but we had to take the risk.

When I talked about Jesus breaking the bread and blessing it, I moved my hand toward theirs. She looked confused because my hand was empty. Her soon-to-be husband whispered, "Just act like it's there. It's invisible." Their hands touched mine, and they put their hands to their mouths and started chewing the invisible wafer. She looked at him out of the side of her eyes like, "Is this the way our marriage is going to start? Are you kidding me?"

All in all, Communion was as good as it was going to get with invisible bread and an empty cup of juice. As I started the next segment of the ceremony, I noticed one of the groomsmen looking down. I wondered if he was going to pass out. It happens. Then I noticed all the groomsmen and bridesmaids looking at the same spot on the floor. It was a lizard. The guys looked amused. The girls were terrified! They wondered if the beast was going to crawl up their legs while they were standing so still. A few seconds later the lizard was on the move. It headed straight for the bride and went under her dress. I tried to make really strong eye contact with her so she wouldn't look down. I think she would have screamed if she'd seen it.

I finished the wedding, pronounced them man and wife, and everybody walked out full of joy. I bit my tongue as long as I could, and then I just burst out laughing. We went to the reception feeling deeply relieved that we hadn't had to call the fire department or animal control. The reception was a lot of fun—but not as exciting as the wedding.

The marriage supper of the Lamb won't be like that at all. It will be perfect, thrilling, and wonderful. Some people—even Christians who have been believers for a long time—assume eternity will be some kind of disembodied existence out there on the clouds somewhere. That's not what the Bible depicts. The new Jerusalem—and the new heaven and new earth—is a physical, tangible place.

The story of God's work began in an actual garden, and it will continue into eternity in a redeemed garden in the city of God. It began with a perfect bride given to Adam, the first man, and it goes into eternity with the perfect bride—the redeemed, restored, resurrected church—given to "the second Adam," our husband, Jesus Christ.

At the marriage supper of the Lamb we'll experience an absence and a presence. Pain, guilt, fear, sorrow, regret, and rage will melt away. They'll all be gone! In their place will flourish joy, love, wisdom, and fulfillment. John described it this way:

> Then I saw a new heaven and a new earth, for the old heaven and the old earth had disappeared. And the sea was also gone. And I saw the holy city, the new Jerusalem, coming down from God out of heaven like a bride beautifully dressed for her husband. I heard a loud shout from the throne, saying, "Look, God's home is now among his people! He will live with them, and they will be his people. God himself will be with them. He will wipe every tear from their eyes, and there will be no more death or sorrow or crying or pain. All these things are gone forever." And the one sitting on the throne said, "Look, I am making everything new!" And then he said to me, "Write this down, for what I tell you is trustworthy and true."
>
> —REVELATION 21:1–5

In Middle Eastern culture the husband would make a grand entrance to take his bride. It was the most dramatic moment of the whole wedding ceremony. The woman would have spent days or weeks preparing for his appearance; he would have dressed in his finest clothes, combed his hair, and wore his nicest cologne (or spices in those days). His groomsmen were his honor guard in the procession to her house. Outside the bridesmaids greeted the entourage and brought her out to him. What will it be like for us to see our husband when He appears to us? It will be utterly breathtaking! Envision the scene John describes:

> Then I saw heaven opened, and a white horse was standing there. Its rider was named Faithful and True, for he judges fairly and wages a righteous war. His eyes were like flames of fire, and on his head were many crowns. A name was written on him that no one understood except himself. He wore a robe dipped in blood, and his title was the Word of God. The armies of heaven, dressed in the finest of pure white linen, followed him on white horses. From his mouth came a sharp sword to strike down the nations. He will rule them with an iron rod. He will release the fierce wrath of God, the Almighty, like juice flowing from a winepress. On his robe and his thigh was written this title: King of all kings and Lord of all lords. Then I saw an angel standing in the sun, shouting to the vultures flying high in the sky: "Come! Gather together for the great banquet God has prepared."
>
> —REVELATION 19:11–17

How do you respond when you see someone who is spectacularly beautiful or handsome? You want to stare, don't you? Of course you do. If you're a woman, you may have daydreamed about opening the door and finding Brad Pitt, Denzel Washington, or Russell Crowe standing there waiting for you. But those guys can't compare to the one John describes—and this isn't a daydream; it's a promise! On that day our mouths will drop open, and we'll gawk at the sight of the King of kings who comes to get us to be His own. He is incredibly handsome, awesomely powerful, and yet full of kindness and love. Do we want justice to right the wrongs we've endured? Out of His mouth is a sword to slay His enemies. His robe is dipped in blood, and the armies of heaven follow Him. The mighty angels of God are His groomsmen! This is the One whom we love—this is the One who loves us and wants us to be His. He is awesome beyond words. What does He say when He comes to our door? "All that I am and all that I have I give to you."

Our hearts almost burst, and we respond, "And all that I am and all that I have I give to You." It's the only reasonable reply to the awesome King who loves us so tenderly, warmly, and fiercely.

When we hear Jesus whisper, "I'm yours and you're Mine," it thrills us, and it changes us forever. We have a new identity—one not based on our talents and performance but on Jesus's declaration of our value. If Albert Einstein said you were smart, you'd have a lot more confidence in your mental abilities. If a great athlete said you were a terrific player, it would put a spring in your step. But here's the deal: the awesome King of kings has chosen you and me to be His bride. I know. It's almost unimaginable, but it's true. He chose you and me on whom to lavish His love. He chose us to share His inheritance of glory, riches, and love. He is coming to our house to pick us up. It's not a mistake. He's the almighty God, full of wisdom and truth. He is making a free choice to make us His beloved bride for the rest of eternity and, as Paul said, to shower us with "the incredible wealth of his grace [favor] and kindness toward us" (Eph. 2:7) for endless days.

THE "ALREADY" AND THE "NOT YET"

Some people who are reading this are a bit confused at this point. They're thinking, "I don't get it. I thought we were already saved, already the bride of Christ, already heirs of the kingdom. What's the deal?"

Good question. The Bible describes a paradox of the "already" and the "not yet." Some of God's promises are fulfilled now, but some won't be completely answered until the scene at the end of Revelation in the new heaven and new earth. For instance, in the Book of Romans Paul wrote that we have "received the Spirit of adoption," but a few verses later he said that we groan, "eagerly waiting for the adoption [as sons]" (Rom. 8:15, 23, NKJV). So which is it? Were we adopted when we got saved, or will we be adopted later when we see Jesus face-to-face? The answer is, "Both." Let me explain:

> We have a new identity—one not based on our talents and performance but on Jesus's declaration of our value.

- *Today* we have the assurance that we've been forgiven, but we still struggle with selfishness and sin. *On that day* all sin will be gloriously gone, and our hearts will be perfectly pure.

- *Today* we have the witness of the Spirit that we're God's beloved children. *On that day* we'll enjoy Him in the perfection of His presence.

- *Today* God is changing us by the power of His Spirit. *On that day* the change will be wonderfully complete.

- *Today* God is giving us wisdom from the Scriptures and discernment by His Spirit. *On that day* we'll no longer look through fogged glass; we'll understand God and His purposes far more clearly.

- *Today* we have the promise of a restored, resurrected body as we feel our bodies fall apart from disease and old age. *On that day* God will give us resurrected bodies like Christ's when He came out of the tomb.

We have wonderful blessings now, but they don't compare to what will come. In his famous sermon "The Weight of Glory," C. S. Lewis explained that we'll experience five things when we meet our husband in glory: we'll be with Christ, we'll be changed to be like Him, we'll experience the true meaning of glory, we'll enjoy the feast, and He'll give us roles to play in the coming kingdom.[1]

These are magnificent truths—so wonderful they're hard to imagine. Paul quoted a passage from Isaiah in his letter to the Corinthians. He wanted to remind a selfish, wayward group of Christians to raise their sights much higher. He wrote them, "That is what the Scriptures mean when they say, 'No eye has seen, no ear has heard, and no mind has imagined what God has prepared for those who love him.' But it was to us that God revealed these things by his Spirit. For his Spirit searches out everything and shows us God's deep secrets" (1 Cor. 2:9–10).

Some might say it does no good to think about our future when there are so many problems today. Jesus, Paul, Peter, the Gospel writers, and the prophets would disagree with that logic. They continually point us to the glorious hope of the future. Dreaming of a wonderful wedding day keeps a bride focused on her fiancé. In the same way, our thoughts about the wedding feast of the Lamb and the consummation of our relationship with Him sharpen our focus. As we rivet our hearts on Jesus, we keep ourselves pure for Him. John used the metaphor of a father and children instead of a husband and wife as he explained our motivation to be pure. He wrote:

> See how very much our Father loves us, for he calls us his children, and that is what we are! But the people who belong to this world don't recognize that we are God's children because they don't know him. Dear friends, we are already God's children, but he has not yet shown us what we will be like when Christ appears. But we do know that we will be like him, for we will see him as he really is. And all who have this eager expectation will keep themselves pure, just as he is pure.
>
> —1 JOHN 3:1–3

Some of us, though, aren't preparing for our wedding day with the King. We're preoccupied with other things, and we seldom think about the One we plan to marry. We can't see Him, so it's easy to put Him out of our thoughts. After all, we have pressing responsibilities, fun to enjoy, stuff to buy, worries to consume our thoughts, hurts to nurse, and all kinds of other distractions. Only days before His arrest Jesus told parables about the kingdom to those who would listen. In one He described ten bridesmaids who were waiting for the groom. During the long delay five of them stayed vigilant. They kept their lamps full of oil so they'd be ready when he arrived. The others, though, got tired and bored. They assumed he wasn't coming, so they went to sleep. When word came that the groom was approaching, they panicked. They ran to get oil for their lamps, but it was too late. Jesus explained the parable: "So stay awake and be prepared, because you do not know the day or hour of my return" (Matt. 25:13, TLB).

Make no mistake: Jesus, our Bridegroom, is coming to get us. In many passages in Scripture the writers describe the event when Christ returns to the earth. He ascended to the clouds in His resurrected body, and He'll return in the same way. But there will be some differences. He came the first time to serve; the next time He's coming back to rule. He came the first time as a baby to grow up and die a horrible death; He's returning as King to bring justice to the earth. Paul explained to the Thessalonians:

> And now, dear brothers and sisters, we want you to know what will happen to the believers who have died so you will not grieve like people who have no hope. For since we believe that

Jesus died and was raised to life again, we also believe that when Jesus returns, God will bring back with him all the believers who have died. We tell you this directly from the Lord: We who are still living when the Lord returns will not meet him ahead of those who have died. For the Lord himself will come down from heaven with a commanding shout, with the voice of the archangel, and with the trumpet call of God. First, the Christians who have died will rise from their graves. Then, together with them, we who are still alive and remain on the earth will be caught up in the clouds to meet the Lord in the air. Then we will be with the Lord forever. So encourage each other with these words.

—1 THESSALONIANS 4:13–18

Are you ready for Him to come back? We don't know when it will be. It could be today, tomorrow, or next year. It's interesting that the people at the church in Thessalonica read Paul's letter about Jesus coming back, and they got discouraged. Why? Because they concluded He had come back and left without them! Paul's second letter assures them that Jesus hadn't returned quite yet. Maybe today; we'll see. But we won't have to guess if it's happened. It'll be the lead story on the news! But then believers won't be around to watch the coverage. We'll be part of the news!

> He came the first time to serve; the next time He's coming back to rule.

AVOID SPIRITUAL ADULTERY

When our love grows cold for any reason in our relationship with God, we turn to other lovers. We commit spiritual adultery. It seldom happens overnight. The slide into the arms of other loves happens gradually, almost imperceptibly. The process parallels the pattern in human relationships. Something relatively minor disappoints us, and we take a step back from God. The distance is fertile soil for doubts about God's goodness and sovereignty, so every new disappointment confirms our suspicions: "See, God doesn't love me."

Nature doesn't like vacuums, so we look for something else to fill the void in our hearts. As we look for substitutes, the things that used to matter don't matter any more. Worship seems dull. The pastor sounds dumb. The Bible doesn't make sense. Going to church is too much trouble. Our Christian friends are so hokey. But now other people and things begin to look much more attractive.

> When our love grows cold for any reason in our relationship with God, we turn to other lovers.

We long for a bigger car, a nicer house, better kids, a more responsive spouse, a prettier figure, more muscles, more lavish vacations, more fun, and all the other things the world promises will satisfy our deepest longings. When these things were only temptations, we said no to them. Now we're saying yes. We trust these people and pursuits to make our hearts sing. They've become our lovers, leaving God out in the cold.

The prophet Jeremiah records a painful conversation.

When God accused His people of spiritual adultery, they barked back, "How can you say that? We haven't pursued other gods!" God responded that it was more obvious than they could imagine. He said that they were like she-camels and wild donkeys in heat, desperate for a lover. When God told them the truth, they changed their story. Now, instead of denials, they rationalized, "Don't bother even talking to me. I can't stop lusting for these things now!" (Jer. 2:23–25).

Doesn't it seem ridiculous for the bride of the King of kings, whom John describes in all His majestic beauty and awesome power, to turn Jesus down and lust after petty, stupid things like popularity, pleasure, and power? It makes no sense at all—if we have even the smallest grasp of Christ's glory, kindness, wisdom, and tender love for us.

Today we live in the tension of God's calling us to love Him with all our hearts and the world's powerful pull to drift away from God to chase after empty promises. Someday we'll have no struggles with sin, but not today. Someday we'll have completely pure motives, but not today. Today we're in a fight. Paul described this conflict in many different ways. To the Galatians he explained:

> So I say, let the Holy Spirit guide your lives. Then you won't be doing what your sinful nature craves. The sinful nature wants to do evil, which is just the opposite of what the Spirit wants. And the Spirit gives us desires that are the opposite of what the sinful nature desires. These two forces are constantly fighting each other, so you are not free to carry out your good intentions.
> —GALATIANS 5:16–17

Some of the guys are thinking, "All right! He's talking about fighting. I can relate to that." A lot of people love the movie *Gladiator*. It shows what it was like to be a gladiator about the time Paul wrote these words to the Galatians. The men chosen for combat in the Colosseum were the best in the business. Experts who were like NFL scouts selected them. Only the best were picked to go through the rigorous training program. I read somewhere that when they were ready to fight, the trainer rubbed them down with oil to make it difficult for the other gladiators to grab them. And they fought naked—no baggy pants and big shirts; no tight workout outfits either. Their adversaries could use their garments as handholds and throw the gladiator down. And if you fell, you were toast.

In the same way, if we want to fight against sin and selfishness in our lives, we have to undress in front of God. He already knows everything about us, but He wants us to come clean with Him and experience His cleansing forgiveness again. Then He pours the oil of the Spirit on us to protect us from Satan's lunges and grabs. We're in a fight—in fact, the fight for our lives—and we need all the protection and advantage we can get.

At the Colosseum, trainers sometimes used an expensive and rare second oil on champion gladiators. It was thicker and had to be worked into the pores. This oil was for the men who had shown unusual bravery in combat. It was an honor and an added protection. The Bible calls this a "double portion." There are times in our lives when we've been fighting a long time, and we don't know if we can go on. If we quit and fall down, we're vulnerable to the enemy's thrust. But if we go back to our trainer, He'll give us a second rubdown of the Spirit's presence and power. Then we're ready to keep fighting.

In any fight, even the winners get banged up, cut, and bruised. And sometimes they get hurt very badly. As we fight for our lover, we suffer from the outside and the inside. We encounter opposition, betrayal, accusations, accidents, and natural disasters. When these happen, we need to remember that God will eventually bring justice and restoration. Through Joel God promised:

> I will give you back what you lost
>> to the swarming locusts, the hopping locusts,
> the stripping locusts, and the cutting locusts.
>> It was I who sent this great destroying army
>> against you.
> Once again you will have all the food you want,
>> and you will praise the LORD your God,
> who does these miracles for you.
>> Never again will my people be disgraced.
> —JOEL 2:25–26

If our problems are caused by our selfishness and sins, God doesn't abandon us. He reminds us that our relationship with Him is based on grace. He has already paid for all of our sins, and He lovingly assures us of His forgiveness. King David (who knew a lot about sin and forgiveness) wrote:

> [God] does not punish us for all our sins;
>> he does not deal harshly with us, as we
>> deserve.
> For his unfailing love toward those who fear him
>> is as great as the height of the heavens above
>> the earth.

He has removed our sins as far from us
as the east is from the west.
—PSALM 103:10–12

Being Christ's bride, then, isn't just about being pretty. We're tender but tough, beautiful but bold. As His bride, we're fiercely loyal to Him. We want to honor Him in everything we do—not because we have to follow some set of rules, but because Jesus deserves every ounce of love in us.

When we get a glimpse of the wedding feast of the Lamb and the glory we'll enjoy one day, we'll devote every hour to love Him, honor Him, please Him, and serve Him. We'll be lovely, secure, strong, and attractive brides when He knocks on the door of our house. We'll be ready.

THINK ABOUT IT...

1. What are some ways a bride prepares for her wedding day? What does a bride hope will happen when the doors open and she sees her man standing in the front to receive her?

2. Read Revelation 19:11–16. Imagine being a bride and having this guy show up at your tent! What would you be thinking and feeling?

3. Describe the "already" and the "not yet" of spiritual promises and experience. Does this concept confuse you or clarify things for you? Explain your answer.

4. How would you define and describe "spiritual adultery"?

5. Why is it important to see our devotion to Christ and our choice to remain pure for Him as a fight?

five

THE BRIDE OF FRANKENSTEIN

I WAS BORN IN New Orleans, but I grew up a few miles up the river in Baton Rouge. I often went with my elementary school friends to the Dalton Theater downtown. On Saturdays the theater had a triple feature. Our parents dropped us off early in the afternoon, and we were there the rest of the day. Our favorite Saturdays were days they showed horror films. The big three were *Frankenstein*, *The Wolf Man*, and *Dracula*. Of course, by the time my generation saw these films, they had all kinds of combinations, including *Frankenstein Meets the Wolf Man*; you can only imagine the titles that could have followed: *Dracula Fights Swamp Thing*, *Godzilla Eats Wolf Man*, and then Dracula invites them all to play cards on Friday night. You get the idea.

The original *Frankenstein* movie was based on Mary Shelley's novel from the early nineteenth century. The film was a huge hit when it came out in 1931, and soon moviegoers were looking for a sequel. Only four years later *The Bride of Frankenstein* hit the screens. Boris Karloff became a legend playing the role of the monster, and millions of kids have dressed up like him on Halloween since that day. In the sequel, Dr. Pretorius creates an artificial brain while his assistant gathers body parts for the monster's bride. The doctor exclaims, "To a new world of gods and monsters!"[1] The plot twists and turns until Dr. Pretorius and his helper create the monster's mate and lower her through the roof to him. Lightning energizes the lifeless female monster, and she stands. Frankenstein is excited and reaches out to her, but she rejects him. The star-crossed monster cries a tear and pulls a lever to destroy the laboratory.

Touching, isn't it? The monster and his bride are dead parts that some evil genius tried to assemble and bring to life with bolts of electricity. They were conceived by man and created by man, and in the end they destroyed those who created them. Frankenstein and his bride are symbols of what's wrong in many of our churches—and in individual hearts—today. There are too many attempts to rearrange dead parts and not enough genuine, trans-formed, supernatural, resurrected life.

Think about it: How does it make any sense at all to spend our time collecting and arranging dead parts when the Lord of life is freely and lovingly offering us a new heart and supernatural transformation? How does it make any sense to strain and strive to try to be good enough to impress God and others—and failing over and over again—when the Spirit of power is waiting to give us the power that raised Jesus from the tomb? How does it make any sense to lie to people and try desperately to win their approval when the Father of glory has adopted us as His own dear children?

We are the glorious and beautiful bride of Christ,

but many of us are acting like the ugly, horrible bride of Frankenstein. Something has to change.

Let me just say it: We're dumb. We think dead body parts (don't think about this image too long) have more potential and are more attractive than a beautiful bride adorned for the One who is about to sweep her off her feet. That's ridiculous, but it's what's going on in countless churches and hearts. We've rejected life, and we've settled for being a dead bride—a stinky one!

SETTLING FOR COUNTERFEITS?

How can we be so misled? Why do we settle for counterfeits? Part of the reason is that our basic human nature insists on independence. The sin in the Garden of Eden wasn't just eating a piece of fruit—it was *the reason* Adam and Eve ate the fruit. They wanted to "be like God"—independent, self-reliant, and in total control. Human beings haven't changed since that day. The history of the world is that God keeps reaching out to invite people to love Him and follow Him in a covenant relationship, but most people look at His outstretched hand and shake their heads, saying, "No thanks. I'd rather do it my way."

> There are too many attempts to rearrange dead parts and not enough genuine, transformed, supernatural, resurrected life.

A second reason people (even people who have said yes to Christ) drift toward other lovers is that our culture is saturated with messages that promise love, fulfillment, comfort, riches, and applause if we just buy this product or use that service. Advertising is based on a huge secondary lie. The toothpaste may clean your teeth, but what's the real, implied promise of the ad? It's that the toothpaste will work magic so that you'll have the man or woman of your dreams. In his insightful book *The Technological Society*, Jacques Ellul observed that advertising creates the false expectation of an ideal life of popularity, affluence, and fun. The problem is that almost everybody believes these assertions. Many people pursue the phantom ideal at the expense of godly values, real relationships, and genuine purpose in life.[2]

The lure of counterfeits and dead parts isn't a modern phenomenon. In Jesus's day two very different groups of people got it wrong. The Pharisees were the right-wingers. They were traditionalists who taught that strict observance of God's rules earns points with God. They had two categories of people: those who were in (themselves) and those who were out (prostitutes, tax collectors, lepers, the sick, foreigners, and anyone else who didn't side completely with them). They hated Jesus because He loved the people they despised. The Sadducees were the left-wing group. They sided with the Romans and compromised their Jewish heritage to get along with the governing authority. They felt threatened by Jesus because He talked about inaugurating a new kingdom—one in which the Romans and Sadducees wouldn't have power. Throughout the Gospels we see these groups arguing with Jesus, testing Him, and eventually plotting to kill him.

In the middle of Matthew's Gospel we find a fascinating conversation between Jesus and His twelve men. Not long before, Jesus had fed five thousand men, not including women and children, with a boy's sack lunch, and He had fed four thousand men plus women and children in a similarly miraculous way. Now the disciples were following Jesus to another town. When it was time for supper, they looked through their bags. Nothing. Nobody had anything to eat, and they worried about going hungry. Jesus saw this as a teachable moment. As they looked at each other and shrugged, He gave them a warning. Matthew (who was there) records the scene:

> "Watch out!" Jesus warned them. "Beware of the yeast of the Pharisees and Sadducees." At this they began to argue with each other because they hadn't brought any bread. Jesus knew what they were thinking, so he said, "You have so little faith! Why are you arguing with each other about having no bread? Don't you understand even yet? Don't you remember the 5,000 I fed with five loaves, and the baskets of leftovers you picked up? Or the 4,000 I fed with seven loaves, and the large baskets of leftovers you picked up? Why can't you understand that I'm not talking about bread? So again I say, 'Beware of the yeast of the Pharisees and Sadducees.'" Then at last they understood that he wasn't speaking about the yeast in bread, but about the deceptive teaching of the Pharisees and Sadducees.
>
> —MATTHEW 16:6–12

In the New Testament, yeast, or leaven, is almost always used as a symbol of evil. Like yeast in a baker's dough, it doesn't take much to make a huge difference! Jesus's disciples hadn't come to some cataclysmic moment in their lives. It was an ordinary day (if you can call any day ordinary when you walk with Jesus), and they had an ordinary problem: they were hungry and needed something to eat. The issue was how they were going to obtain it. Would they trust in their own efforts and resources, or would they reflect on the clearly and recently demonstrated power of Jesus and trust Him to provide? We face this choice dozens of times every day. Our decisions reveal what's in our hearts.

The presence of evil, unbelief, and arrogance poisons everything it touches. When Paul wrote the Corinthians, he had to address a long list of problems. He had to tell them that God values sexual purity. He warned them to avoid doing business with the temple prostitutes, but that wasn't all. He heard that a man was having sex with his stepmother! I'm sure the guy rationalized it as completely normal. That's one of the ways we avoid dealing with our sins. The people in Corinth were amused by the man's behavior. Paul wasn't. He was outraged. When he wrote them about this problem, he pointed them back to the night when God told His people to bake unleavened bread, sacrifice a lamb, and put its blood on the doorposts of their houses. Paul explained:

> Your boasting is not good. Don't you know that a little yeast works through the whole batch of dough? Get rid of the old yeast that you may be a new batch without yeast—as you really are. For Christ, our Passover lamb, has been sacrificed. Therefore let us keep the Festival, not with the old yeast, the yeast of malice and wickedness, but with bread without yeast, the bread of sincerity and truth.
>
> —1 CORINTHIANS 5:6–8, NIV

How is the yeast of sin addressed? By throwing out the whole batch, trusting in the sacrifice of the lamb, and cooking a new batch of unleavened bread—a life of purity, sincerity, and truth. This kind of action requires boldness. Apathy or confusion won't cut it.

The bride of Christ becomes the bride of Frankenstein when it has any or all of four traits: hypocrisy, unbelief, impurity, and legalism. To mix our metaphors, these are the leaven of evil—the dead body parts that can't make a live, beautiful bride. The bride of Christ is full of love, joy, forgiveness, kindness, and generosity, but the characteristics of spiritual death produce competition, anger, fear, self-pity, and delight in finding fault in others. Dead parts can't be put together by human efforts to produce something beautiful. Frankenstein's bride was ugly…really ugly. And many churches today are just as dead and ugly. Like Frank and his honey, many churches have dead parts—lifeless pastors, teachers, leaders, and members. On Sunday morning it looks Boris Karloff and the Clones are up front leading music. And like Frankenstein and his bride, many churches are terrified of fire—not their church burning down, but their church becoming holy fireplaces where the Spirit enflames people with love, beauty, and power.

We can't look the other way any longer. We can't settle for a collection of dead parts. We don't want to be monsters; we want to be a beautiful bride. For us to change, we have to be honest when we look into

> The bride of Christ becomes the bride of Frankenstein when it has any or all of four traits: hypocrisy, unbelief, impurity, and legalism.

the laboratory and see parts that are dead. Let's look at these traits of the bride of Frankenstein.

HYPOCRISY

Luke tells us that Jesus specifically warned His followers, "Beware of the yeast of the Pharisees—their hypocrisy. The time is coming when everything that is covered up will be revealed, and all that is secret will be made to all. Whatever you have said in the dark will be heard in the light, and what you have whispered behind closed doors will be shouted from the housetops for all to hear!" (Luke 12:1–3). In the Roman and Greek world people understood the word Jesus and Luke used for hypocrisy. In Greek plays actors wore masks in the theater. The word *hypocrisy* comes from the Greek word for an actor's mask. Hypocrites wear masks to hide their true motives and appear noble and pure. The Pharisees were all about the exterior. They wore nice robes, went to the finest banquets, and jockeyed for the best seats. But they didn't stop there. They believed they were one-up on others. Everything was competition, and they were determined to be the winners. They put themselves on pedestals, putting down anyone who didn't measure up to their standards. Sound familiar? Hypocrites in churches do the same things today. They make a point of looking holy, sounding holy, and acting holy—not because they see themselves as beautiful brides of Christ, but to be one-up on their competition in the next pew.

> We have to realize the masks we wear are attempts to lie to God and to other people about the true condition of our hearts.

The Pharisees had seen almost everything Jesus had done. He hadn't been living in a closet. They saw Him turn water into wine, raise people from the dead, cleanse lepers, heal the sick, calm storms, cast out demons, and restore paralyzed people to full health. How did they respond? Instead of getting on their knees in wonder and worship, they felt threatened and were determined to kill Jesus.

Still, Jesus didn't hate them. He loved them. One of the most poignant moments in the Gospels is at the end of the parable about the prodigal son. The elder brother in the story represents the Pharisees. He's angry, resentful, and full of self-pity. When his wayward brother (who represents the prostitutes and tax collectors) repents and comes home, his father (God) welcomes him, forgives him, reinstates him, and throws a lavish party to celebrate! The elder brother, though, is so furious at his father's display of forgiveness and love for his brother that he won't come to the party. The parable ends with the father going outside to plead with the angry son to come in and celebrate. Jesus's point was clear: God was inviting the angry, resentful, hypocritical Pharisees to repent and join the party of God's love and grace. They didn't. A few weeks later they killed Jesus.

Some hypocrites in the church have at least a twinge of remorse for being arrogant and judgmental. They sometimes quickly tell God, "I'm so sorry." But they don't change. It takes more than a glimpse of sin to change a life. We have to realize the masks we wear are attempts to lie to God and to other people about the true condition of our hearts. Paul said, "God's kindness leads you [us] toward repentance" (Rom. 2:4, NIV). When we look at the matchless love and kindness of Jesus, our hearts melt. We don't want to miss out any longer, so we admit our hypocrisy and bask in the glow of His grace. Then, with new motivation and desire, we genuinely repent. The beauty of Christ becomes our beauty. We love the unlovely, forgive offenders, reach out to care for those who can't give us anything in return, and give generously. And we do it all without a thought for acclaim. We do it for an audience of one.

When I talk to people on the streets, in stores, or at games, I hear one thing over and over again about the church: "It's full of hypocrites." They don't mean, "The church is full of struggling people." They would understand and accept that fact. No, they're upset because too many people in the church have dark hearts and deceptive practices, but they put on masks that try to project purity and nobility. They see churches—and church people—that are totally dead and terribly ugly. The bride of Frankenstein is full of hypocrites. Unbelievers see the truth, and they're repulsed. If we want to reach people, we have to take off our masks and be real—which means we have to be honest about the sin in our lives and repent. We need to become people who are good at confessing and repenting. That's what the world is looking for. That's what Jesus is looking for too.

> The beauty of Christ becomes our beauty.

The grace of God isn't an excuse to deny our sin; it's an invitation to be ruthlessly honest about our blatant sins as well as our secret ones. Repentance happens in a moment, but it's also a process. In an instant we choose to turn from selfishness to generosity and kindness, but we have hundreds of choices to make before the new pattern becomes a habit. We get a picture of *the instant* and *the process* when we read the account of King Hezekiah taking the throne. The nation was in shambles. The wickedness of King Ahaz had ruined the land and its people. When Hezekiah took over, he immediately commanded the priests to cleanse the temple so God's people could worship the Lord in glory, wonder, humility, and truth. His command took only moments, but the process of cleaning out the filth took time, effort, and determination. This is how the chronicler describes it:

> These men called together their fellow Levites, and they all purified themselves. Then they began to purify the Temple of the LORD, just as the king had commanded. They were careful to follow all the LORD's instructions in their work. The priests went into the sanctuary of the Temple of the LORD to cleanse it, and they took out to the Temple courtyard all the defiled things they found. From there the Levites carted it all out to the Kidron Valley. They began the work in early spring, on the first day of the new year, and in eight days they had reached the entry room of the LORD's Temple. Then they purified the Temple of the LORD itself, which took another eight days. So the entire task was completed in sixteen days.
>
> —2 CHRONICLES 29:15–17

How does God cleanse us from hypocrisy and selfishness? Through an instantaneous decision and a process of repentance. We stop denying our sin, and we stop excusing ourselves for hurting others. We bring our deepest, darkest sins out into the bright light of God's holiness, and there we find abundant grace. John explained, "If we claim we have no sin, we are only fooling ourselves and not living in the truth. But if we confess our sins to him, he is faithful and just to forgive us our sins and to cleanse us from all wickedness" (1 John 1:8–9). God is "faithful and just" to forgive us because Jesus has already paid the price for every sin. Our confession doesn't merit God's forgiveness; it makes God's grace, love, and cleansing real to our hearts.

UNBELIEF

The second trait of Frankenstein's bride is unbelief. The Pharisees were the most religious people on the planet, but they failed the first requirement: to look at Jesus and believe in Him. Nicodemus was one of their leaders. He was curious about Jesus, so he asked to meet with Him. He didn't want anybody to see him with this strange teacher, so he asked Jesus to meet him at night. When Jesus talked to him about the spiritual reality of being born of the Spirit, Nicodemus didn't have a clue what He was talking about. For three years the Pharisees heard Jesus teach and watched Him perform miracles, but their hearts still didn't believe what their eyes saw and their ears heard. At the end only one of them, Joseph of Arimathea, was at the cross to take down the body.

> Repentance happens in a moment, but it's also a process.

The Sadducees had a different problem. They were secularists who didn't believe in the supernatural. When Paul was on trial in Jerusalem after his third missionary trip, both groups, the Pharisees and Sadducees, accused him of being disloyal to the Jewish faith. He split their alliance by pointing out the Sadducees' faulty faith. Luke tells us about the debate:

> Paul realized that some members of the high council were Sadducees and some were Pharisees, so he shouted, "Brothers, I am a Pharisee, as were all my ancestors! And I am on trial because my hope is in the resurrection of the dead!" This divided the council—the Pharisees against the Sadducees—for the Sadducees say there is no resurrection or angels or spirits, but the Pharisees believe in all of these. So there was a great uproar. Some of the teachers of religious law who were Pharisees jumped up and began to argue forcibly. "We see nothing wrong with him," they shouted. "Perhaps a spirit or an angel spoke to him."
>
> —ACTS 23:6–9

Today, many in our churches are like the Sadducees: they're secularists who see the church as a civic club with no supernatural purpose or power. To them there are no God-sized goals, no sense of wonder in worship, and no trust in the Spirit's power to do miracles. When there's no faith in the supernatural presence and power of God, we're left with rules, pleasant chatter, and broken lives with nothing to fix them.

Jesus had worked miracles as signs of His divinity and evidence of the coming kingdom. God had healed people when Peter's shadow passed over them (Acts 5:15), and handkerchiefs from Paul had been infused with the Spirit's healing power (Acts 19:12). God is still in the business of healing bodies and changing hearts. He's still a miracle-working God.

Many in our churches, though, don't believe God exercises power any more. Oh, He may have done it years ago in Creation and through Jesus, but no longer. They have effectively become deists. They think God spun the universe into existence and then took His hands off. They claim, "You can't really believe all that stuff. You have to be rational." That's exactly what the Bible wants us to be: rational. If you believe God has the power to create the universe and the love to send Jesus to die for us, it's entirely rational to believe He's still involved in our lives.

It's odd, isn't it? People can go to church week after week, sing songs of faith and hear messages about God's awesome power and love, but they walk away as if they'd just attended a seminar on graveyard etiquette. Here's a news flash: Yes, Jesus was dead. He was in the tomb and completely dead, but three days later He came out in His resurrected body! He was gloriously alive, and He still is today! If we don't believe He's alive, we can't have a relationship with Him. All we have are nice songs, bland platitudes about how to be nice people, and a powerless life. The writer to the Hebrews assures us, "Jesus Christ is the same yesterday, today, and forever. So do not be attracted by strange, new ideas. Your strength comes from God's grace, not from rules about food, which don't help those who follow them" (Heb. 13:8–9).

When Jesus sent the disciples out two by two, God used them to heal diseases and cast out demons. After the Spirit fell on the people on the Day of Pentecost, they saw God do many miracles of healing. Today God is waiting for His people to believe Him to do amazing things in the lives of people around them—and their own lives. He's not finished showing His strength.

Some Christians aren't comfortable with the way other believers trust God to work. Denominations argue about what God did years ago and what He's doing today. At one point John complained to Jesus that somebody wasn't casting out demons in the right way. Jesus responded, "Don't stop him!...No one who performs miracles in my name will soon be able to speak evil of me" (Mark 9:39). I'm not concerned about the fine points of doctrine and practice. It doesn't matter to me if people cast out demons with a power encounter or a truth encounter. The issue isn't technique; it's a profound and vibrant faith in the presence, purpose, and power of Almighty God!

> A pure substance can become impure with just a small amount of impurity added.

A lot of people aren't comfortable with miracles because it makes them feel out of control. Well, yeah, that's the point. Our lives are a wreck, and we need God to step in with His power and love to fix what's out of control. We can't make Him do what we want Him to do, and we can't stop Him from doing what He insists on doing. But there is the statement by Jesus that He did only a few miracles because of their unbelief (Matt. 13:58). Think about it: Is God being hindered because of people's rationalizing and lack of faith in your church—and maybe in you?

IMPURITY

The third trait of Frankenstein's bride is impurity. It's not that every Christian is a thief, coward, sex addict, and murderer. A pure substance can become impure with just a small amount of impurity added. That was Jesus's point when He talked about yeast—a little goes a long way.

Think of it this way: You have a glass of sparkling clean water. How much of another person's spit, mud, or bug guts does it take for you not to drink it? Not much, and probably not any. In Paul's letter to the Colossians he talks about the need to get rid of every impurity, but he begins by reminding us about our motivation. The lustful lure of earthly things can't compare to the beauty of our Savior and husband. He wrote:

> Since you have been raised to new life with Christ, set your sights on the realities of heaven, where Christ sits in the place of honor at God's right hand. Think about the things of heaven, not the things of earth. For you died to this life, and your real life is hidden with Christ in God. And when Christ, who is your life, is revealed to the whole world, you will share in all his glory.
>
> So put to death the sinful, earthly things lurking within you. Have nothing to do with sexual immorality, impurity, lust, and evil desires. Don't be greedy, for a greedy person is an idolator, worshiping the things of this life. Because of these sins, the anger of God is coming. You used to do these things when your life was still part of this world. But now is the time to get rid of anger, rage, malicious behavior, slander, and dirty language.
>
> —COLOSSIANS 3:1–8

It's not that God wants to take the joy out of life—He wants to take the sting out of life. God gives restrictions to protect us from harm. The things that are off limits are poison. The problem, of course, is that the labels we read on those bottles promise love, joy, pleasure, wealth, power, and popularity. A lot of those things—sex, money, friends, family, and fun—are perfectly good. In fact, they're gifts from God, and He wants us to enjoy them to the fullest— as long as they stay secondary instead of primary. When they become idols, they become poison. And some are always destructive. Even a little greed, lust, rage, gossip, and filthy talk ruin us and our relationships.

Have you ever seen meth addicts? Gradually the impact of the drug causes devastating effects on their bodies. Their teeth rot, their skin gets pockmarked, and they lose weight. They look like death. They look like Frankenstein or his bride. That's the way a lot of us look to our neighbors, family, and friends. They may not know what impurity is our addiction of choice, but they see the effects: we're ugly and repulsive.

> God gives restrictions to protect us from harm. The things that are off limits are poison.

How can we know if some part of our lives is impure? Here are some signals:

- We hide some behaviors from our spouse, kids, friends, and employer.

- We can't stop thinking about getting and having that thing. It becomes an obsession.

- We spend too much money and time on it.

- People tell us we're out of balance in that area, but we laugh them off.

- The Holy Spirit has convicted us over and over again, but we've ignored Him.

Purity isn't following a set of rules. That's being a Pharisee! The kind of purity God wants for us is like a woman who is completely devoted to her fiancé. She can't imagine anyone else who could captivate her. She is completely his, and he is totally hers. Their devotion is pure, deep, and strong. Fierce love is the source of godly purity.

LEGALISM

The fourth characteristic of the monster's bride is legalism, which is an ethical system that measures a person's acceptance with God by the level of compliance to "the rules." These people are devoted to obedience—not to a loving God who has won their hearts, but to a set of rules and regulations so they can show God and others they're good enough to be accepted. They may talk about God, but their hearts aren't really His at all. They're going through all the religious motions to prove themselves. Of course, they also measure other people by how well they keep the rules. They compete with each other, argue about which rules are most important, and delight when the other person stumbles. Sounds like fun, huh?

People have all kinds of measuring sticks for themselves and each other. They look down their noses at people who don't wear the right clothes, don't raise their hands in worship, raise their hands in worship, speak in tongues, don't speak in tongues, miss a service once in a while, read a new translation of the Bible, use particular words, dance, drink, chew, spit…the list is endless. The problem is that these rules divide people and create modern-day Pharisees who don't really care about Jesus at all. Does that sound harsh? When was the last time you overheard Christians complain about each other in a gossip session?

The church in Colossae had problems with legalism. A faction of people in the church had drifted away from the gospel of grace and were trying really hard to measure up (and they were sure the others weren't measuring up!). Paul corrected them:

> Don't let anyone condemn you by insisting on pious self-denial or the worship of angels, saying they have had visions about these things. Their sinful minds have made them proud, and they are not connected to Christ, the head of the body. For he holds the body together with its joints and ligaments, and it grows as God nourishes it.
>
> You have died with Christ, and he has set you free from the spiritual powers of this world. So why do you keep on following rules of the world, such as, "Don't handle! Don't taste! Don't touch!"? Such rules are mere human teachings about things that deteriorate as we use them. These rules may seem wise because they require strong devotion, pious self-denial, and severe bodily discipline. But they provide no help in conquering a person's evil desires.
>
> —Colossians 2:18–23

When legalists hear people like me warn them they're missing the point of the gospel, they bristle, "Well, you don't care about obedience! Jesus values obedience, but you obviously don't."

Actually, I care a lot about obedience, but I care just as much about the motivation as the behavior. When we focus on just the behavior, we use it as a club to beat people into submission, and we use fear and guilt on ourselves to keep us from straying away from the rigid, straight line of rules. Rules without grace motivate us to look very religious, but they "provide no help in conquering a person's evil desires." Rules alone make us monsters. Grace-motivated obedience makes us loving, caring, compassionate, tenderhearted, and noble. Your pick. Don't blow it.

Man-made religion may produce attractive programs and nice buildings, but it lacks the qualities of real life: love, delight, and passion. It tries to look pretty, but it's horribly ugly. Frankenstein and his Mrs. weren't good at social skills. They had only one friend. His name was Igor, and he wasn't invited to many birthday parties. People in dead churches (and dead people in churches that are alive) are often superficially friendly, but they don't really love the unlovely. They may regularly attend service, but their hearts are seldom stirred in awe and worship. They settle for being respectable, but they're afraid of what might happen if the fire of the Spirit was turned loose among them.

Many of Jesus's fiercest confrontations were with religious leaders who insisted on defending the dead, religious status quo. Over and over again Jesus taught them, performed miracles, and pleaded with them to turn from their rigor mortis of the soul to experience His life and love. They refused. In one particularly tense encounter when the Pharisees kept opposing Him, Jesus told them, "Why can't you understand what I am saying? It's because you can't even hear

> Rules without grace motivate us to look very religious, but they "provide no help in conquering a person's evil desires."

me! For you are the children of your father the devil, and you love to do the evil things he does. He was a murderer from the beginning. He has always hated the truth, because there is no truth in him. When he lies, it is consistent with his character; for he is a liar and the father of lies. So when I tell the truth, you just naturally don't believe me!" (John 8:43–45). What would Jesus say to many of our churches today about our resistance to the fire of His Spirit? What would He say to you and me?

Two passages in the New Testament are shocking statements that expose the bride of Frankenstein. In His most famous sermon Jesus described two types of trees, two kinds of foundations for houses, and two motivations for prayer, fasting, and giving. The distinction between the two isn't what we might think. He wasn't talking about good people and bad people, obedient people and flagrant sinners. He was describing two people who are sitting in church on Sunday morning. His words are chilling: "Not all who sound religious are really godly people. They may refer to me as 'Lord,' but still won't get to heaven" (Matt. 7:21, TLB). These people were prophesying, casting out demons, and performing miracles. They were doing wonderful ministry, but they were doing so with dark hearts. Jesus said to them, "I never knew you" (v. 23).

The second passage is similar, but the apostle Paul penned this one. We often read the thirteenth chapter of his first letter to the Corinthians at weddings and write it in calligraphy for our walls. But have we ever noticed the first part of it? Paul is talking about the preeminence of love as our motivation, and he says it's possible to be involved in all kinds of good things without being driven and directed by God's amazing love. We can speak in tongues, prophesy, move mountains with our faith, and give everything we have—including our bodies in death—but if these things don't come out of hearts overflowing with love for God, they're worth absolutely nothing (1 Cor. 13:1–3). Both Jesus and Paul were describing the bride of Frankenstein—people who look alive on the outside but are dead on the inside. We shouldn't pass too quickly over these arresting passages. They are written to cause us to say, "Wait a minute! What are my motivations? Am I involved in good things for the right reasons, or is it all just a sham, a mask to cover up the deadness inside?" These are good questions. Remember: It's not about following rules, impressing people, or earning points with God. It's about experiencing the life-changing love of God and becoming truly alive to Him.

When people looked at Jesus, what did they see? He is the only person who has ever kept the rules perfectly, but is that what people talked about? No, they marveled at how much He loved people. When people look at the church, do they see a bunch of people who are more committed to rules and blasting people who don't follow them? Who would want to join something like that? Jesus didn't. He started a revolution. He invites people to admit they can't follow the rules. When they embrace Him as their Savior, He transforms their hearts by His grace, and then they want to obey Him. It's a radical theory...one that has changed the world.

No Longer a Monster

The great news is that the bride of Frankenstein doesn't have to remain a monster. Through the miracle of grace God can change her into His living, gorgeous bride. Being beautiful isn't based on how big our buildings are, how many people attend, how much money a person gives, the style of music, or anything else on the outside. The church becomes beautiful when each individual believer confesses and repents from hypocrisy, unbelief, impurity, and legalism.

When a couple gets married, they make a positive affirmation and a negative one. They say "You're mine and I'm yours" to each other, but they also are saying, "I don't belong to anyone else, and you don't belong to anyone else." In the same way we need to say no to the traits of Frankenstein's bride, but that's not enough. We need more. We need a lover to ravish our hearts. We need Jesus to capture our souls, enthrall us, and take us away with Him. We respond by loving Him with all we have—body, mind, heart, soul, and strength. We aren't flippant, and we don't take Him for granted. Jesus becomes our greatest treasure, and we adore Him.

When we love God like this, amazing things happen. God trusts us with the power of His Spirit, and He is set loose among us. Dead parts don't exhibit life. They just lie there and rot. But a living, beautiful bride is the center of attention. Every eye is drawn to her, and people delight in her expressions of joy as she talks about her man. That's what evangelism is: people watch us and hear us as we delight in Jesus. As the beauty of Jesus captivates us, He gives us His heart, and we become beautiful. How in the world does that work? We have to go to the beauty parlor.

THINK ABOUT IT...

1. What are some ways Frankenstein's bride is like the modern church? Is that comparison too harsh? Why or why not?

2. Why do people wear masks? What are they afraid of showing? What kind of security is necessary for people to be honest about what's really going on in their lives?

3. Why do we rationalize unbelief? Why does authentic, strong faith in Jesus make some people feel threatened?

4. What kinds of impurity do people most easily excuse? What are the long-term effects of putting up with impurity?

5. What are some evidences of legalism? Why does it seem so attractive to so many people? What's the cure?

6. Describe the good, right, and biblical motivation for obedience.

six

THE BEAUTY PARLOR

THE EXTREME MAKEOVER for the bride of Christ begins in two unlikely places: the hematologist's office and the morgue. The blood coursing through the veins of the bride of Frankenstein isn't the cleansing, healing, loving blood of Jesus; it's pride and fear. That's what makes her strong and nasty. She thrives on the arrogant assumption that she doesn't need anybody. She's independent, self-assured, and one-up on everybody. When she goes to church, she's not going to bow in humble adoration. Not at all. She's going there to earn points with God and people, and to learn principles she can follow to climb one more rung up the ladder to prove she's better than other people. But in her more lucid moments she knows she can't measure up, so she's haunted by the fear someone will see her mask slip, that they'll see her ugliness in all its shame.

Pride and fear are fuels that drive these people to all kinds of self-destructive behaviors (ones that also hurt those around them). Arrogance and terror produce a wide variety of actions, including jealousy, compulsive drives, apathy, rage, bitterness, worry, addictions, distractions, and the pursuit of riches, approval, and power. We may think this list describes people who are in prison or are terrible sinners, but they are in the hearts of people in the row next to us on Sunday morning—and if we're honest, we notice evidence of them when we look in the mirror.

CHRIST'S CLEANSING BLOOD

The blood of Jesus cleanses us from all these sins—and all the rest. His love gives His bride security and thrills her soul! His blood "make[s] the vilest sinner clean,"[1] redeems, restores, and imparts real life. When His blood is our fuel, we're swept up in His beauty—"lost in wonder, love, and praise."[2]

People with blood disorders look pale and weak. We can't imagine them running a marathon or winning a beauty pageant. In the same way, the diseased spiritual blood of pride and fear makes us look sickly and unattractive to those around us. When the blood of Jesus refreshes and empowers us, it shows! We aren't distracted by worries and lusts for more power, applause, and possessions. We're as lovely as a bride on her wedding day. Everyone notices! And everyone wants to hear our story of love and devotion.

We need to remember that we're in a spiritual battle. As long as Satan can deceive us to believe that the empty distractions of the world are more valuable than Jesus, we'll pursue them instead of Him. We'll daydream about having more and better stuff, and we'll drift away from Christ. In Paul's second letter to the Corinthians, he made a dramatic statement. Paul was the ultimate tough guy. He went to city after city to preach the gospel. As he approached each one, he was well aware that he faced almost inevitable attacks: verbally, legally, and physically. People tried to kill him! He seemed to be utterly fearless, but one thing made him afraid. He wrote, "But I fear that somehow your pure and undivided devotion to Christ will be corrupted, just as Eve was deceived by the cunning ways of the serpent" (2 Cor. 11:3). If Paul was afraid that the Corinthians would be deceived and distracted, what would he say about us? The bride of Christ who is thrilled with His love has a "pure and undivided devotion to Christ." We won't be completely free from pride and fear until we see Jesus face-to-face, but the more we know and love Him, the more our devotion will be pure and undistracted.

Receiving New Life

The second strange place where we start our beauty treatment is the morgue. (No, ladies, I'm not really recommending this as a new technique for you. It's just an analogy, so stay with me.) We could go to many different passages of Scripture that explain the miracle of God breathing new life into spiritually dead people, but we're going to start and stay in Paul's letter to the Ephesians. The picture he paints of people sounds like Frankenstein's bride before she's electrified. He explained:

> Once you were dead because of your disobedience and your many sins. You used to live in sin, just like the rest of the world, obeying the devil—the commander of the powers in the unseen world. He is the spirit at work in the hearts of those who refuse to obey God. All of us used to live that way, following the passionate desires and inclinations

of our sinful nature. By our very nature we were subject to God's anger, just like everyone else.

—EPHESIANS 2:1–3

Pretty bleak, isn't it? Notice this: Paul isn't saying people are *as bad as they can be*. They may not be murderers, rapists, or child abusers. But they are *as bad off as they can be*—hopeless and helpless, without any way of twisting God's arm or earning points...destined for eternal destruction.

Two of the most wonderful words in the Bible follow Paul's somber depiction of the human condition: "But God..." What did God do to rescue us? He didn't demand that we jump through hoops to prove we're worthy. He knows we're not worthy and can never be worthy on our own. Paul says that God performs a miracle of bringing dead people to life:

> But God is so rich in mercy, and he loved us so much, that even though we were dead because of our sins, he gave us life when he raised Christ from the dead. (It is only by God's grace that you have been saved!) For he raised us from the dead along with Christ, and seated us with him in the heavenly realms because we are united with Christ Jesus.
>
> —EPHESIANS 2:4–6

If that doesn't give you goose bumps, you're probably still dead.

Jesus—our lover, husband, King, and friend—showers His grace on us. His grace isn't *un*conditional; it's *counter*-conditional. It's not that we don't deserve His love, forgiveness, and acceptance; it's that *we richly deserve* condemnation and punishment for eternity—but He has lavished His grace on us instead. To make his point, Paul unveils more of God's heart. What are God's intentions? "So God can point to us in all future ages as examples of the incredible wealth of his grace and kindness toward us, as shown in all he has done for us who are united with Christ Jesus"

> Jesus's grace isn't *un*conditional; it's *counter*-conditional.

(v. 7). For time and eternity He points to us as His gorgeous bride, and He's proud to call us His own!

Paul is well aware that grace is one of the most misunderstood concepts in the world. We "say grace" before meals, and we "give people grace" when we look the other way when they've hurt us. Grace is much more than that. It's not just a prayer, leniency, or a good feeling. It's a sacrificial payment made out of a heart of love. A preacher once defined grace as "**G**od's **R**iches **A**t **C**hrist's **E**xpense." To make sure we get it, Paul continued explaining grace to his readers (including us): "God saved you by his grace when you believed. And you can't take credit for this; it is a gift from God. Salvation is not a reward for the good things we have done, so none of us can boast about it" (vv. 8–9).

Is that overkill? Did Paul need a good editor to keep his letter from repeating the same point? No, the concept of grace is so important that he doesn't want us to miss it. It's the antidote for the poison of pride and fear—the *only* antidote.

Jesus's grace brings dead people to life, and it makes us incredibly beautiful. In the opening chapter of the letter to the Ephesians Paul uses extravagant language to describe what God has done to us, in us, and for us. God wasn't stingy with His grace. He lavishly poured out His wonderful kindness to us in Christ. He knows everything about us—all our arrogance, fear, and self-pity—but before the foundations of the earth were laid, He chose us to be His beloved bride and planned to adopt us to be His dear children. He forgave all our sins, "purchas[ing] our freedom with the blood of his Son [Jesus]." To confirm our new life and new relationship, God sent His Spirit to whisper to our spirits that we belong to Him. Paul says the Holy Spirit's presence in our lives today is a "guarantee." Other translations say it's a "down payment" or "earnest." This means there's a lot more to come (Eph. 1:1–14).

Here's the way Paul describes the Spirit's role in our lives today:

> And now you Gentiles have also heard the truth, the Good News that God saves you. And when you believed in Christ, he identified you as his own by giving you the Holy Spirit, whom he promised long ago. The Spirit is God's guarantee that he will give us everything he promised and that he has purchased us to be his own people. He did this so we would praise and glorify Him.
> —EPHESIANS 1:13–14

Do you struggle with arrogance and the need to be one-up on people? God's grace humbles you to the dust. Do you wrestle with feelings of fear and self-doubt? God's grace raises you to the stars! It reverses the world's value system. The ones who think they have it made on their own are out, and the ones who are humble enough to realize they're sinners get in. Because of the cross of Christ, dead and ugly people become alive and beautiful! We have a radically new identity. When we look in the mirror after the beauty treatment of God's truth and grace, we feel good about ourselves! We're brand-new. Old things have passed away, and the new has come! We have a spring in our step, new confidence, and a heart filled with joy.

Do you belong to a church where this kind of grace is loudly proclaimed? Or is grace an afterthought for people who are determined to prove themselves to God and people—modern-day Pharisees? One of the marks of a church of grace-filled people is love for one another. It doesn't just happen. Left to ourselves, we create divisions and struggle with feelings of inferiority and superiority. In the celebration of God's amazing grace, everybody is valuable, and everybody is welcome!

In our day people draw boundaries along lines of race, ethnicity, culture, gender, and age. In the first century the first Christians had the same tendency to draw a circle around people like them and exclude everyone else. The sharpest distinction was between Jews and Gentiles, with the biggest question being: Can Gentiles become Christians? Paul had an answer. The temple in Jerusalem had several different rooms and courts. The holy of holies was the smallest and most sacred space. The high priest went in once a year to offer sacrifices for the sins of God's people. Outside it was the holy place, the courts for men, and still farther out, the court for women. At the farthest extremity of the temple was the court of the Gentiles—the ones who had chosen to follow the true God but weren't Jewish by birth. The priests had built a wall around the court of the Gentiles to keep them separate—and to remind them they were second-class believers. This distinction was recognized throughout the Roman Empire in the Jewish synagogues. Separation had become the cultural norm, but it wasn't acceptable to God for His church. Paul explained that the gospel of grace pulverizes the wall between races and ethnic groups. He wrote:

> For Christ himself has brought peace to us. He united Jews and Gentiles into one people when, in his own body on the cross, he broke down the wall of hostility that separated us. He did this by ending the system of law with its commandments and regulations. He made peace between Jews and Gentiles by creating in himself one new people from the two groups. Together as one body, Christ reconciled both groups to God by means of his death on the cross, and our hostility toward each other was put to death.
> —EPHESIANS 2:14–16

You might read this and reply, "That's cool. It's ancient history that has nothing to do with me, but it's cool." You couldn't be more mistaken. It has everything to do with the divisions we've created between groups of Christians. We make a federal case about almost anything: the type of music, the form of worship, the racial profile of people where we do outreach, people sitting next to us, the color of those on the platform, age, gender, ministry philosophy, wealth, politics, and everything else imaginable. People have created denominations to keep their friends in and others out. We have designer churches for white people, African American people, Hispanic people, Asian people, old people, young people, enthusiastic people, and reserved people. Pick your group and exclude the rest. Paul said that superiority and inferiority, suspicion and exclusion, don't reflect the love of God for His bride. When we find walls between people, we tear them down in Jesus's name. When we see hostility between people, we put it to death by showering people with the sacrificial love demonstrated on the cross. We realize we have an identity that transcends all the things that separate people—the love of Jesus bridges all gaps and heals all wounds. It enables us to look deep into people's souls and love them for who they are. That kind of love changes lives. That kind of love is a brilliant light shining in a dark world.

I've preached in some churches about the grace of God, but hearts were hard. People were more interested in building walls than tearing them down. I preached my heart out to explain the love, forgiveness, and power of Jesus, but people just sat there in stony silence. When I talked to people in these churches, I heard stories of bickering, factions, backbiting, vicious gossiping, and sheer delight in putting others down. These churches aren't growing. Do you know why? Because God isn't going to put a healthy baby in a rancid, dirty, stinking incubator. He's a good parent. He loves His new babes in Christ, so He's going to put them in a place where they will be nurtured and supported—not a perfect church, but one that's full of honest, loving, growing people. And of course, people who are just exploring faith certainly aren't going to be attracted by the stench of discord in those churches! People who haven't yet found Christ are much more attracted to the sweet fragrance of believers who love Jesus and each other.

Unity and love aren't optional equipment in God's

family. They're essential. Throughout this short letter to the Ephesians Paul comes back again and again to the importance of unity. But we can't manufacture it. It has to happen in response to the grace of God. Paul doesn't let up. At the turning point in his letter he explains that the grace God has worked *into* us naturally and powerfully flows *out*. What does the overflow of God's love and power look like? It looks like unity:

> Therefore I, a prisoner for serving the Lord, beg you to lead a life worthy of your calling, for you have been called by God. Always be humble and gentle. Be patient with each other, making allowance for each other's faults because of your love. Make every effort to keep yourselves united in the Spirit, binding yourselves together with peace. For there is one body and one Spirit, just as you have been called to one glorious hope for the future. There is only one Lord, one faith, one baptism, and one God and Father, who is over all and in all and living through all.
>
> —EPHESIANS 4:1–6

This kind of love between different groups and classes of people doesn't automatically happen. It's a work of the Spirit, and God uses loving and gifted leaders to create the environment for growth and change. Godly, loving leaders model inclusion, teach grace, and help people take steps of repentance and care. Paul explained:

> God isn't going to put a healthy baby in a rancid, dirty, stinking incubator.

[The leaders'] responsibility is to equip God's people to do his work and build up the church, the body of Christ. This will continue until we all come to such unity in our faith and knowledge of God's Son that we will be mature in the Lord, measuring up to the full and complete standard of Christ.

—EPHESIANS 4:12–13

Social theory and good theology are important, but they aren't good enough to build true unity of the Spirit. People need to make a hundred choices each day to say no to selfishness and exclusivity and say yes to loving God and people. Paul compares these choices with changing clothes. When I change clothes, the clean ones don't magically pounce on my body. I have to intentionally take off the dirty duds, take a bath to wash off the sweat and dirt, and purposefully pick out and put on clean clothes. In our lives the process of change looks like this:

- First, we notice we're wearing dirty clothes. We realize we're selfish, hateful, judgmental, sarcastic, and arrogant... or afraid, apathetic, timid, bitter, and withdrawn. When we see these traits, Paul tells us to "throw off your old sinful nature and your former way of life, which is corrupted by lust and deception" (v. 22).

- To have better motives and choose loving actions, our minds and hearts have to change. We need to think God's thoughts and share His values. As we focus on Him and His priorities, we trust His Spirit to transform us from the inside out. Paul wrote, "Instead, let the Spirit renew your thoughts and attitudes" (v. 23).

- And finally, with new thinking about God's amazing grace, our new identity, and God's purposes for us, we make new and better choices. We "put on" new behaviors. Paul explained that we "put on [our] new nature, created to be like God—truly righteous and holy" (v. 24).

Paul didn't let people off the hook by letting them think they could stay in the abstract in their obedience to God. He gave them a series of choices to put off sinful habits, let the Spirit renew their minds, and put on new, God-honoring choices: Stop lying; instead tell the truth. Stop letting selfishness fuel anger; let your anger propel you to protect the innocent. Stop stealing; instead work and share with others. Don't use filthy language; always use words that build people up. Get rid of bitterness; be kind, loving, and forgiving—and treat others the way Christ has treated you.

Is that practical enough for you?

Yet Paul is not finished with giving instructions for relationships; he keeps going back to the heart motive. He reminds us:

Imitate God, therefore, in everything you do, because you are his dear children. Live a life filled with love, following the example of Christ. He

loved us and offered himself as a sacrifice for us, a
pleasing aroma to God.

—Ephesians 5:1–2

When our hearts are enthralled with Jesus, we make
different choices. We don't want anything to offend the
one we love! People in the Roman world had problems
with things that sound familiar to us today: sexual immo-
rality, impurity, greed, obscene stories, foolish talk, and
coarse jokes. Have you watched television lately? All of
these sins entertain us! Paul tells us not to even tolerate
darkness because "now you have light from the Lord. So
live as people of light!" (v. 8).

In this letter Paul keeps digging deep into our human
connections and shows how the gospel of Christ transforms everything. He gives directions to husbands and
wives, children and parents, bosses and employers. In all
of these he points us to
Christ's loving sacrifice as
the motivation to love, the
example to serve, and the
power to obey.

First he addressed
wives. He has just spent
a lot of time in the letter

> Paul didn't let
> people off the hook
> by letting them think
> they could stay in
> the abstract in their
> obedience to God.

describing the love of God and the power of the Spirit to
make all of us humble and loving. In this context he tells
wives: "For wives, this means submit to your husbands
as to the Lord. For a husband is the head of his wife as
Christ is the head of the church. He is the Savior of his
body, the church. As the church submits to Christ, so
you wives should submit to your husbands in everything"

(Eph. 5:22–24). Paul is not advocating an oppressive, male-dominated relationship. He's saying that love, tenderness, humility, and compassion should characterize each person, but the buck stops with the husband. On those rare occasions when they've talked about an issue but still disagree, the wife is to submit to her husband's leadership in the same way she submits to Jesus. Her husband thrives on her respect, and she thrives on his love and affection. That's where Paul is going next.

Paul compares a husband's love for his wife with Christ's sacrifice and passion for His church. He wrote: "For husbands, this means love your wives, just as Christ loved the church. He gave up his life for her to make her holy and clean, washed by the cleansing of God's word. He did this to present her to himself as a glorious church without a spot or wrinkle or any other blemish. Instead, she will be holy and without fault" (vv. 25–27). How are wrinkles removed from a shirt? With an iron...a hot iron. Bringing passion back to a stale marriage doesn't happen if the husband stays cool and distant. His love for God and his wife have to be reignited! He needs to burn with white-hot love—first with the love of Jesus for him, then with love for Jesus, and finally with a renewed love for the woman God has given him. A lot of men (and women) prefer to remain chilled and isolated because real passion feels threatening. That's their choice, but if they want a marriage based on biblical principles, they have to go to the cross, experience the joy and delight of Jesus's love, and then let that love overflow to each other. We can choose to remain numb, cool, and distant, but this decision adversely affects every other relationship in our lives—with our kids, our friends, our church, and our

Lord. We all have wrinkles, and we need God's hot iron of love, conviction, delight, and power to iron them out. Nothing else will do.

Many parents and kids today feel as if they're living in a video game in their homes—lots of attacks and defensive maneuvers to get advantage over each other, but there's too much collateral damage! Parents are often preoccupied with worries at work, distractions in the community, and misplaced dreams for themselves and their children. Parents tend toward one of two extremes: being too involved, controlling their kids' lives...or backing off and letting the children fend for themselves. And quite often one parent goes one direction and the other parent the reverse. It's a mess.

Paul speaks into this distress:

> Children, obey your parents because you belong to the Lord, for this is the right thing to do. "Honor your father and mother." This is the first commandment with a promise: If you honor your father and mother, "things will go well with you, and you will have a long life on the earth." Fathers, do not provoke your children to anger by the way you treat them. Rather, bring them up with the discipline and instruction that comes from the Lord.
>
> —EPHESIANS 6:1–5

Or, in twenty-first-century terminology: "Kids, remember that you belong to the Lord, so obey your parents because your love and loyalty honor your parents and the Lord. This is the first command with a promise of a long, meaningful life. And parents, stop exasperating your kids by either being a helicopter hovering over them to smother them with attention or vanishing from their daily lives and leaving them alone when they need you most."

Parents have the God-given privilege and responsibility to give their children two indispensable things: roots and wings. Kids need roots of a strong, stable, loving family so they can try their wings of creativity and increasing independence as they grow from adolescence into adulthood. Just as the Lord trusts us with more responsibility as we mature spiritually, parents need to trust their kids (as they earn it) with more flexibility and responsibility. The parents' goal is to launch their children to college, marriage, or the working world with a firm foundation of faith, confidence, wisdom, and love. That's what beauty looks like in our children's lives.

In his instructions for people in businesses, Paul actually was addressing masters and slaves. In that day most slaves were temporarily indentured servants, not kidnapped and permanently enslaved people. Paul reminds servants-slaves-employees to work as if Jesus is their boss: "…with deep respect and fear. Serve them sincerely as you would serve Christ. Try to please them all the time, not just when they are watching you. As slaves of Christ, do the will of God with all your heart. Work with enthusiasm, as though you were working for the Lord rather than for people. Remember that the Lord will reward each one of us for the good we do, whether we are slaves or free" (vv. 5–8). Paul points both labor and management to Jesus. He tells masters and employers, "Masters, treat your slaves in the same way. Don't threaten them; remember, you both have the same Master in heaven, and he has no favorites" (v. 9).

What would it look like if these relationships were characterized by the love and power of Jesus? We'd be spectacularly attractive! We'd stand out like a lighthouse in our communities! We'd be a beacon of hope for broken marriages, prodigal children and their parents, wounded employees, and stressed employers!

In the middle of his directives about relationships, Paul explains that we can't do all this in our own strength. Some people think they just need to try harder to live the Christian life. When they fail again and again, they feel lousy about themselves. They either double down to try even harder, or they give up in despair. There's another way: we can be filled with the Spirit. How can we know we're filled with the Spirit? Paul gives a few evidences: We sing with joy—spontaneously or with others. We overflow with gratitude for all God is to us and has given us. And instead of jockeying for positions of power and winning applause, we display humility by submitting to each other "out of reverence for Christ" (Eph. 5:16–21).

From the Morgue to the Battlefield

Paul ends this powerful letter with the familiar passage describing the armor we wear in spiritual warfare. It's interesting, isn't it? We began the beauty treatment in the morgue, and we end it on the battlefield. God hasn't called us to live as a beautiful trophy on a pedestal. We get down into the trenches and fight by His side for His honor and His cause—rescuing a lost world from sin, death, and hell. But notice that Paul has spent much of the letter focusing on how the grace and love of Jesus break down walls between people, stir love, and overflow into each other. He writes about unity before he writes about combat. Too often we try to reach *lost* people before the *found* people demonstrate love for each other. If we don't have a loving, warm, supportive environment in the church, why would a loving Father put babes in Christ in our care? He wouldn't, and He doesn't...at least, not very often.

People used to say, "Charity begins at home." Evangelism begins when we clean up our relationships in the church and our families and choose to love each other. Before Jesus left the earth from the hillside, He instructed the disciples, "But you will receive power when the Holy Spirit comes upon you. And you will be my witnesses, telling people about me everywhere—in Jerusalem, throughout Judea, in Samaria, and to the ends of the earth" (Acts 1:8). In some of our congregations, resentment and fear are so thick that they've poisoned the church's reputation in the community. If they want to have an impact, they first need to look inside and do the hard work of confession, repentance, restoration, and restitution. They have to start where they are. No excuses, no blame shifting. Just ruthless honesty and humble repentance. In the same way Jesus told the disciples to start where they were—in Jerusalem. It would have been easier to start somewhere else. After all, Jerusalem was where the religious elite and the Roman government had conspired to kill their Savior! Jerusalem was where the fickle crowd had yelled "Hosanna to the King" when Jesus rode in on donkey's colt but a week later screamed,

> Too often we try to reach *lost* people before the *found* people demonstrate love for each other.

"Crucify Him!" A lot of those people were still around! And Jerusalem was the site where some of them had made their most foolish blunders. Peter had denied he even knew Jesus, and all but John had run like scared schoolgirls when Jesus was arrested. Jerusalem was a scary place for the followers of Jesus.

But it was precisely there that God wanted to work the miracle of faith, hope, and love. Jerusalem was the home of the Jewish religion and culture, and it was the birthplace of the church ten days later when the Holy Spirit came upon the 120 in the Upper Room. It was dangerous, but it was the place where God wanted to reveal Himself in power and love.

God wants to do the same thing in our churches today. Many of them are just as dangerous as Jerusalem in the days after the crucifixion—full of doubt, intrigue, gossip, betrayal, resentment, and fear. If God could work His miraculous power in Jerusalem to create a loving, supportive community, He can do it anywhere! And if God can work a miracle in our churches to replace bitterness with love and suspicion with trust, the whole world will sit up and notice.

Will we look beyond petty differences to reach out to one another in genuine love and care? When we major on the minors, we make molehills into mountains. Will we reject gossip and bickering so we can have real dialogue and build bridges of trust? We have a real choice to stay ugly or become beautiful.

People are watching. They want to see if Jesus is real in us or if it's all just a game. We can't manufacture Christ's beauty. He has to produce it in us as we drink deeply of His presence, power, and pardon. That's the pattern of spiritual life: we become more *loving* toward others as Jesus's love floods our hearts (1 John 4:10–11). We reach out and *accept* people who are different or annoying only when we've experienced Jesus's counter-conditional acceptance (Rom. 15:7). And we *forgive* those who hurt us to the extent that we're amazed that Jesus has forgiven us for our selfishness, betrayal, pride, and cowardice (Eph. 4:31–32). The beauty of Christ is the direct result of looking intently at Jesus and being amazed at His magnificent beauty.

Some time ago I visited someone from our church who had been rushed to the emergency room at the hospital. As I waited to see him, a frantic lady came through the doors. She announced to anyone who would listen, "A boy…a boy was riding his bike! A car hit him. They're bringing him in right now."

At that moment two men came in carrying the limp body of the boy. Someone had called his mother, and she hurried in a minute later. When she saw her son, she burst into tears. The boy was unconscious. The nurses quickly took him back for the doctor to see him. They asked his mother to stay outside while they examined him. They assured her they'd come get her as soon as they could. When the big doors closed, the mom cried uncontrollably. I walked over to her and asked, "Can I help you? Is there anything I can do for you?"

She sobbed, "My son was just hit by a car. I don't know what's wrong with him, and they won't let me see him!"

I asked, "Do you have a pastor you want me to call?"

She shook her head and cried again at the thought of being helpless and alone.

I said, "I'm a pastor. My church is right down the street."

Her eyes brightened, and she exclaimed, "Padre! I'm so glad you're here!"

Padre? Close enough. I didn't care what she called me, and I didn't bother to define theological points at that moment.

I told her, "They'll probably let me back there as they examine him. I can pray for him, and then I'll come back and tell you what's going on. Do you want me to do that for you?"

She grabbed me and hugged me really tight. She said, "Padre, would you please do that for me?"

I could barely breathe, but I replied, "I'll be glad to."

I went back to the examining rooms and found the boy and the doctor who was examining him. He had regained consciousness and was coherent. The doctor told me the boy had a broken leg, but he was going to be fine. I prayed for the boy, his mother, and the doctors.

When I came back to give the good report to his mother, she couldn't have been happier if she'd won ten lotteries. She gave me a big hug and burst into tears— tears of joy this time. She asked, "You prayed for him, Padre?"

"Yes," I assured her. "I prayed for your son, and I prayed for you too." By this time several other family members had joined her in the waiting room. I asked, "Can I pray for your family?"

She nodded. She gathered her family, and we held hands. The room wasn't designed for a prayer meeting, so we had to step around some chairs so we could all hold hands in a circle. I prayed for God's blessings on this dear family. I didn't use the moment as an opportunity to invite them to church, and I didn't go through the gospel and have an altar call right there in the waiting room. It wasn't the right time for that. I just was present with some compassion and care. I know one thing: this mom and her family won't forget what happened that day. If anybody ever said anything bad about the pastor of The House/ Modesto, she would have slapped him on the side of the head! I had become a trusted friend to her.

Most of us have no idea how powerful it is to offer to pray for someone. Time after time Deborah and I have prayed for people in trouble. We don't teach them systematic theology, and we don't give them a discourse on the history of the church. We simply show up and offer to talk to Almighty God for them. Sometimes people aren't saved before we pray for them, and they may not be saved after we pray. We have no idea how God will answer our prayers. Some of these people have showed up days, weeks, or months later at our church to tell us they got saved. They gave us big hugs and thanked us for taking their needs to God.

In the moment of this mother's desperate need, I simply showed up and offered to help. She didn't screen me to see if I fit her theological grid, and she didn't analyze my résumé to see if I had the experience to fit a preconceived expectation. She simply felt desperate, and I offered to help. That's the nature of love. She was thrilled someone— anyone!—would step into her life to care for her and her beloved son.

Prayer. It's incredibly powerful. Paul often included brief prayers in his letters to the churches. In this letter to the Ephesians he doubled up. His first prayer is in the first chapter. He told them, "I have not stopped thanking God for you. I pray for you constantly, asking God, the glorious Father of our Lord Jesus Christ, to give you spiritual wisdom and insight so that you might grow in your knowledge of God. I pray that your hearts will be flooded with light so that you can understand the confident hope he has given to those he called" (Eph. 1:16–18).

As God opens the eyes of our hearts to grasp the wonder of His love, He answers this prayer by giving us three insights: a wonderful sense of hope, a deep realization of how rich we are because of God's grace, and the experience of the incredible greatness of God's power— the same power that raised Jesus from the dead!

In his second prayer Paul asks God to overwhelm us with His love: "May you experience the love of Christ, though it is too great to understand fully. Then you will be made complete with all the fullness of life and power that comes from God." Paul ends this prayer with an explosion of praise, worship, and wonder. "Now all glory to God, who is able, through his mighty power at work within us, to accomplish infinitely more than we might ask or think. Glory to him in the church and in Christ Jesus through all generations forever and ever! Amen" (Eph. 3:19–21).

When God answers these prayers for you and me, phenomenal things happen in our hearts and in our relationships. We delight in Jesus so much that our cares and worries don't drag us down any longer. We *feel* rich beyond comprehension because we finally grasp the fact that we *are* rich beyond comprehension. And the Holy Spirit courses through us to give us the power to love people and see miracles accomplished: marriages restored, prodigals returning, and broken hearts mended.

That's what the world longs to experience. They've been looking at us, the church, to see if that's what we experience in our relationship with Jesus. If it is, many will flock to join us—just as five thousand joined the church in Jerusalem in the first weeks after Pentecost. People want to see believers who have been made staggeringly beautiful by the transforming love of Jesus Christ. But first, we have to go to the beauty parlor. Paul showed us what that means. Have you been? Are you ready?

THINK ABOUT IT...

1. When pride and fear dominate a person's life, what are some of the results (in the individual's life and relationships)?

2. Read Ephesians 2:1–10. Why does grace require us to be honest that we are utterly helpless and hopeless—dead, in fact—apart from God's life-giving mercy, grace, and love? What does it cost to be this honest with God?

3. How do arrogant people think about themselves? How do ashamed people think about themselves? Read Ephesians 1:3–14. What difference does it make for both kinds of people to realize they're chosen, adopted, forgiven, and sealed by the Holy Spirit?

4. Do you agree or disagree with this statement: God's grace humbles you to

the dust, and it raises you to the stars!
Explain your answer.

5. How does our new identity in Christ
affect relationships in the church, our
families, and at work? What are some
practical ways the experience of Jesus's
beauty breaks down walls between
people?

6. Think about everything in Paul's letter
to the Ephesians. How would you sum-
marize how he described the way God
makes us beautiful?

7. Read Paul's prayers in Ephesians
1:15–23 and 3:14–21. Pick one and
paraphrase it as your own prayer to
God. Whom are you thinking about as
you pray it?

seven

WHEN DOES CHURCH START?

WHAT IS WORSHIP? Some pastors get upset when parishioners say, "The worship was really good, and I enjoyed the sermon too." The pastors try to explain, "Yeah, but the sermon is part of worship too!"

But that's still not accurate. Worship isn't limited to the first part of a church service, and it's not even the whole service. Worship is a lot bigger than that. In fact, worship is our commitment to the thing or person who captures our hearts, energizes us, and makes our lives worth living. And it's not just for Christians. Everybody worships something. Every person on the planet has determined that something is so valuable it's worth their whole lives. They may not say these exact words, but if you listen closely, they say something like:

- My life only has meaning if my children love me.

- My life only has meaning when I'm in a romantic relationship.

135

- My life only has meaning if I have enough money. (Well, more money than that guy!)

- My life only has meaning if I achieve a certain position in my company.

- My life only has meaning if I am free, independent, and can do whatever I like.

- My life only has meaning if the right people respect me.

- My life only has meaning if I'm beautiful or handsome.

- My life only has meaning if my team is winning.

- My life only has meaning if I've followed all the rules so no one can find fault in me.

We could go on and on, but you get the idea. A lot of people sitting in churches every Sunday don't believe Christ has ultimate value. They come to church with the hope He'll help them achieve success in their other pursuits. To them, Jesus is a means to their ends—not the greatest, most wonderful, magnificent treasure the world has ever known.

Think about it. Jesus is the Creator of the universe and the sustainer of all that exists. Sure, He was a baby at one point, and He lived and died as a man, but in the mystery of faith, He was Almighty God incarnate. We get a glimpse of the greatness of Christ when we look at what He created. If the distance from the earth to the sun (about 93 million miles) is represented by a single sheet of paper, the distance to the nearest star would require a stack of paper 71 feet high. Our Milky Way galaxy is just an average one among about 200 billion galaxies in the universe. (Yeah, I wish it was one of the best and biggest, but it's not. Too bad. Can we get into another one?) The diameter of our galaxy would require a stack of paper 310 miles high! And the distance to the edge of the known universe (about 14 billion light-years away) would need a stack 31 million miles tall![1] Jesus—the One we pray to and sing about—is the One who spoke a word and created all this. He didn't sweat at all. Is this the kind of person we should be treating like a waiter? Is this the one we think we should tell how to run our world? Is this the one we can take for granted?

No; this is the One we should fall down and worship. His greatness is far beyond anything we can ever imagine, and His love is deeper than the deepest sea.

When does He love us and have a plan for us? All

> Everybody worships something.

day every day. Where does He rule? Everywhere. The only reasonable response is to tell Him, "You are magnificent! I belong to You, and it's my highest honor to represent You everywhere I go." So when does church start? It doesn't begin and end on Sunday morning at a particular time. We *are* the church, and we *never stop being* the church. In everything we are, everything we do, and everywhere we go, we belong to the King of kings, our treasure and our beloved husband. Church starts right here right now, and it never ends.

THOSE GOD CALLS

We need to remember that God hasn't called the cool people, the well connected, the rich, and the popular to represent Him. Jesus invited the outcasts and the misfits to join Him in building His kingdom. And He still invites the same kind of people—those who have enough self-perception to know they're dead, helpless, and hopeless without Jesus's blood and the power of the Spirit—people like you and me. Through Isaiah God called out, "Sing, O childless woman, you who have never given birth! Break into loud and joyful song, O Jerusalem, you who have never been in labor. For the desolate woman now has more children than the woman who lives with her husband" (Isa. 54:1).

In ancient Jewish culture barren women were at the bottom of the social ladder. Women only had status if they had children—and the more the better. If women were childless, people assumed God had cursed them. In this passage in Isaiah the woman represents God's people who haven't been following Him. They've been disobedient, faithless, and wayward. But God hasn't given up on them. They may feel worthless, but God still reaches out to them with a sweeping plan:

> Enlarge your house; build an addition.
> Spread out your home, and spare no expense!
> For you will soon be bursting at the seams.
> Your descendants will occupy other nations
> and resettle the ruined cities.
> —ISAIAH 54:2–3

People who wandered lived in tents. God was saying, "Get ready to make a difference in your community! You're going to have to expand to make room for all the people I'm going to bring in! And they're going to be people you birth into God's kingdom." It was like telling us, "Knock the walls out of your living room. Make it really big! I'm going to use you to reach a ton of people with the love of Jesus!"

The exiles who originally read these words would have responded like many of us: "It's too late. No, not me. I'm too far gone. God can't use me. I'm pathetic. Go find somebody else." But God assured them:

> Fear not; you will no longer live in shame.
>   Don't be afraid; there is no more disgrace for
>   you.
> You will no longer remember the shame of your
>   youth
>   and the sorrows of widowhood.
> For your Creator will be your husband;
>   the LORD of Heaven's Armies is his name!
> He is your Redeemer, the Holy One of Israel,
>   the God of all the earth.
>   —ISAIAH 54:4–5

Shame and disgrace paralyze people. They cause us to focus on ourselves instead of God and His purposes, they erode our energy, and they leave us wallowing in self-pity. God is saying, "Snap out of it! You're better than that! Yeah, you've blown it, but I've forgiven you. Yes, you've made a mess of things, but I have the wisdom and power to turn ashes into beauty [Isa. 61:3]. And you don't have to do this alone. Remember: the Lord of the universe [the one we described a few paragraphs ago] is majestic in love and power. I'm your redeemer and your husband. You can trust Me!"

So, if your problem is pride, compare your puny talents and smarts to Almighty God. You lose, but He loves you and wants to use you. If your problem is oppressive shame and low self-esteem, the Lord of glory loves you and calls you His own. It doesn't get any better than that!

It's easy to become complacent. We get comfortable with just enough money, just enough pleasure, just enough excitement, and just enough spiritual life. At times God has used this passage to say to me, "Glen, I have more for you...a lot more! Enlarge your tent. Move the stakes out...way out. Don't bother Me with excuses. Just trust Me. I'm a lot bigger than your doubts. Remember who I am, Glen. I'm about to do something you've never seen before. In fact, you've never even imagined it!"

I'm a fearless guy, but if I allow fear a foothold in my life, it paralyzes my thinking, hinders my prayers, creates divisions in relationships, and destroys my joy. If left untreated, fear is like a wasting disease that slowly (or not so slowly) kills my dreams. When fear captures me, I focus on the ways people have hurt me and disappointed me instead of living in hope for a wonderful future of God's blessings. Can you relate?

The reminder of our calling as Christ's beloved bride restores our security and confidence. It humbles us because we remember we don't deserve His incredible love, and it stimulates us to dream big dreams to spread His fame around our communities and the world! Our new identity raises our vision and changes our self-perception. We move from being a spectator to a soldier, from a critic to a servant, and from a complainer to someone who pours his life out for others. When the love of Jesus captures our hearts, we can't sit still! We kneel to pray, we get up and shout, and we get our hands busy helping others.

The abundant life isn't having more stuff and more fun. It's making a difference for God and His kingdom! I think the Holy Spirit would say to many of us, "I'm living in you, but I'm tired of sitting with you as you watch television for hours and hours. I'm bored when you waste time watching meaningless movies and reading books that don't inspire you. I'm embarrassed when I hear you gossiping about people instead of loving them and helping them. I have a lot more for you than fun, diversions of entertainment, and daydreams about sex or vacations or promotions or whatever. I want to use you to change people's lives! I'm ready to use you in the classroom, at the office, over the back fence with your neighbors, or in the bleachers. I want to use you in all parts of town—and all parts of the world—but you'll never go if you remain stuck in your selfishness. You're a new creation—act like it! You're the bride of the King—honor Him!"

JOY: ESSENTIAL AND NONNEGOTIABLE

God wants to take us on an exciting adventure, but many of us are distracted by things that don't matter at all. We go to church to check off our list that we've done our religious duty for the week (or to get our spouse off our backs). We may read the Bible and pray a little, but our goal is to earn some points with God so He'll give us what we want. We have a Prozac religion designed to numb the pain. We have a Dr. Phil faith to make us feel better about ourselves. We have a fast-food spirituality to fill us up quickly so we can get on with "more important things." When we live like this, we drift away from our first love, our highest purpose, and our deepest joy.

Joy is an essential ingredient in the abundant life, and it's a nonnegotiable if we're going to look beautiful to those who are watching us. Joy is the natural explosion of being assured we're loved. The bride and groom almost burst with joy as they see each other in the church. A mother quickly forgets the pain of childbirth as she holds her dear baby in her arms. She's radiant with joy! The problem is that many Christians seem allergic to joy. They try to stay as far away from it as possible! When they stand before the Lord after they die or when the Rapture happens, God will ask them, "I gave you a lot. Did you have a good time?"

They'll kind of tilt their heads and grimace a bit as they say, "Well, not exactly. Things didn't go the way I wanted them to. (And by the way, where were You? I asked You to bless me. Didn't You hear my prayers?) Come to think of it, my life has been more like getting stuck in a dentist's chair! I hated it. It was horrible. I couldn't wait to get out of there!"

Joy isn't the same thing as happiness. Being happy is conditional. We need pleasant circumstances to experience happiness. Genuine joy is categorically different. It's a sense of delight, hope, and security that can't be shaken by difficulties. It's not that we become immune to heartache—ours or anyone else's—but there is something deeper, something richer, something weightier than the hardships or benefits we experience. We have the profound certainty that the mountains may shake, but the

Creator still rules; the markets or our jobs may falter, but God is still on His throne. The enemy may throw everything in hell against us, but we set our minds on things above, not on those below. Satan attacks us from the left and the right, the top and the bottom. We encounter opposition and deception at home, at work, and with our friends. His scheme is to get us to take our eyes *off* the beauty of Jesus and *on* the ugliness of the world. Joy says, "No, I'm going to keep looking to Jesus and His infinite love, power, and beauty!" Real joy isn't the absence of conflict but the victory we experience *during* conflict because our faith enables us to endure. And we experience joy *after* the conflict because we celebrate with the One who gave us hope and strength!

People around us are watching to see how we respond to difficulties. Most people react to problems in one of three ways: fight, flight, or freezing up. Some people bow up, get angry and loud, and fight back against any perceived threat. Fear pulls the trigger of aggression. These individuals believe they have to dominate through intimidation. Others have the opposite reaction: they run as fast and as far as they can! They can't wait to get out of the room, out of the office, and maybe out of town. They spend their lives trying to avoid the people and situations that have caused them pain—and might cause more pain in the future. A third kind of person is the one who becomes emotionally paralyzed. These people don't fight and they don't

> Real joy isn't the absence of conflict but the victory we experience *during* conflict because our faith enables us to endure.

143

run; they freeze up. When they feel stressed and you ask them to make a decision (even a simple one), they shrug, "I don't know."

How do you respond in difficult circumstances? What do people see when you are going through hard times? Do you fight back, run away, or become paralyzed in fear and hopelessness? Or do people see you trusting God and digging deep to experience real joy even when the world is crashing down around you? In these times those who are watching don't want to hear you speaking "happy talk" with a senseless smile on your face. Your authentic faith enables you to be ruthlessly honest about the situation and your pain, but you still have a rock-solid faith that God is good and He's still on His throne.

David wrote many of the psalms. He was a warrior and a poet, fierce and reflective. In one of his psalms he explained the source of true joy:

> You faithfully answer our prayers with awesome
> deeds,
>   O God our savior.
> You are the hope of everyone on earth,
>   even those who sail on distant seas.
> You formed the mountains by your power
>   and armed yourself with mighty strength.
> You quieted the raging oceans
>   with their pounding waves
>   and silenced the shouting of the nations.
> Those who live at the ends of the earth
>   stand in awe of your wonders.
> From where the sun rises to where it sets,
>   you inspire shouts of joy.
>   —PSALM 65:5–8

God answers our prayers, but not always with comfort and plenty. Sometimes He shows Himself strong by stilling a raging storm and sometimes by silencing a warring nation. We can count on God coming through—in His way and in His timing—in an obvious way so that people all over the world will marvel at Him. What will be their response? Shouts of joy!

Later in the psalm David tells God, "You crown the year with a bountiful harvest; even the hard pathways overflow with abundance" (v. 11). All the time and in all areas of our lives God brings overflowing blessing. Sometimes it's in material goods, but it's always in spiritual riches. The love, forgiveness, power, and presence of God are ours all day every day, in good times and in bad, no matter what happens. The greatest blessing is God's very presence. We may not sense Him, but He's there. We may pray and not realize He's listening, but He hears every word. The light around us may have become dark, but God is right there with us in all of His glory, kindness, and strength. This assurance gives us confidence in our most difficult moments. It's the source of unending joy. When we have this security, we can face anything with honesty, courage, and yes, real joy.

The joy of the Lord, Nehemiah told us, is our strength (Neh. 8:10). We don't get this joy by trying harder, manipulating situations, or avoiding pain at all costs. It comes from a spiritual transformation—a beauty treatment—by the Holy Spirit's work deep in us. For many Christians, the Spirit is the forgotten member of the Trinity. He points us to Jesus, and He honors the Father. Without the Spirit we'd be dead in the water: no hope, no power, and no purpose. The Spirit leads us to discover "the deep things of God" (1 Cor. 2:10, NIV). I often pray, "I welcome You, Spirit of God, because I desperately need You. Show me the deep things. Open my heart to grasp the wonder of Your love, and give me a vision of how I can serve You and honor You. You are the instrument of harmony and unity as I relate to other Christians. You open the eyes of the blind to grasp the gospel. You use my arms to care for the needy and my feet to bring food and freedom. You use my words to inspire hope for those with broken hearts."

No Lone Rangers in the Kingdom

Without the Spirit of God, I'd be just like every other "younger brother" speeding toward self-indulgence and ruining his life, or like all the other "elder brothers" who delight in condemning people instead of reaching out in grace and love. Only the Holy Spirit gives us the power to change to become a little more like Jesus: welcoming sinners, sacrificing for those in need, being patient with annoying people, freeing those in bondage, feeding the hungry, reaching out to the millionaires and the home-less, building relationships with the noble and the pros-titutes, genuinely loving the homosexuals and foreigners, and trusting God to accomplish great things for His kingdom—with a humble heart and no strings attached. No, we can't do that on our own.

To be the people God wants us to be, we need hearts filled with the beauty and power of the Spirit, but we also need each other. No one can be a Christian alone. This statement has many meanings. First, very few people come to Christ without the personal involvement of someone who cared enough to tell them the gospel of grace. And no one grows in his faith in isolation. God created us as relational beings. To thrive, we need Him, and we also need each other. Where is the church? It may have a specific address where people meet on Sundays and for other gatherings, but the church exists wherever God's people rub shoulders—at school, at the mall, in offices, in living rooms, in stadiums, in coffee shops, and everywhere else imaginable. The church isn't confined to a structure; it travels with you and me wherever we go.

Many years ago I was sound asleep in the middle of the night when God woke me up. I sensed Him say to me, "Glen, in most churches I'm unemployed. I'm capable and available. Would you put Me to work in the lives of every believer in your church?" Who would have thought that God would see Himself as unemployed and applying for a job? But that's the way it is. He's standing outside our churches knocking on the doors asking, "Will you use Me? I have skills and experience. Will you allow

> No one can be a Christian alone.

Me to transform you and make you beautiful? I'm available to work any shift. Do you need to see My résumé? It's the Bible. Yeah, it's kind of long, but it shows that I've had a lot of experience. Just let Me know if you'd like Me to come to work."

The Spirit doesn't want part of us; He wants all of us. We don't need God to be our waiter or butler; we need Him to be our Savior and King. We don't worship Jesus for an hour on Sunday and a few minutes each day in devotionals (if that); we belong to Him and represent Him all day ever day. A dab of Jesus won't do!

A prophetic passage in Ezekiel gives us a graphic image

of what it means to go deeper in our faith. The prophet wrote:

> In my vision, the man brought me back to the entrance of the Temple. There I saw a stream flowing east from beneath the door of the Temple and passing to the right of the altar on its south side. The man brought me outside the wall through the north gateway and led me around to the eastern entrance. There I could see the water flowing out through the south side of the east gateway. Measuring as he went, he led me along the stream for 1,750 feet and then led me across. The water was up to my ankles. He measured off another 1,750 feet and led me across again. This time the water was up to my knees. After another 1,750 feet, it was up to my waist. Then he measured another 1,750 feet, and the river was too deep to walk across. It was deep enough to swim in, but too deep to walk through. He asked me, "Have you been watching, son of man?" Then he led me back along the riverbank.
>
> —EZEKIEL 47:1–6

Notice the progression. At first the prophet was only ankle-deep in the water. A lot of people today are shallow in their walks with Jesus. They barely get their feet wet in praise, thanksgiving, obedience, and service. As long as church is fun, they come. When they read the Bible or pray, they think they're doing God a favor. They don't get much out

> The church isn't confined to a structure; it travels with you and me wherever we go.

of sermons because they're thinking about what they're going to do that afternoon. When someone asks them to help, they may pitch in, but not for long. It's just too much trouble, and it interferes with their favorite shows on television.

The prophet crosses the river again, but this time, he's up to his knees. Some people are more involved, but they're not wet up to their wallets! They want to keep complete control over their money, and they aren't too sure what God wants in their relationships, time, and habits.

Ezekiel crosses the river a third time, and now he's up to his waist. At this level of devotion and involvement people are more intentional, and the current of the Spirit has more control of their lives, but their hands and heads are still free, and their feet can still touch the bottom. They've given God lordship over certain parts of their lives, but they're still guarding something too precious to them to give to Him. They're still in control of their lives.

Finally, the prophet is in over his head! He's swept away by the current of the river—fully engaged, fully under the water's control. This is what Paul was talking about when he told us to continually "be filled with the Holy Spirit" (Eph. 5:18). And this is the kind of commitment Jesus described when He told His disciples, "If any of you wants to be my follower, you must turn from your selfish ways, take up your cross, and follow me. If you try to hang on to your life, you will lose it. But if you give up your life for my sake, you will save it. And what do you benefit if you gain the whole world but lose your own soul? Is anything worth more than your soul?" (Matt. 16:24–26). Nothing held back. No half-measures. Like the guy playing Texas Hold'em would say, "I'm all in!" We say to God, "I love

You more than anything and anybody. I'm Yours. All I am is Yours, and all I have is Yours. My family, my career, my finances, my health, my hopes, my future—it's Yours. You've given it all to me, and I gladly give it back. Your love and beauty amaze me!"

In Ezekiel's vision something dramatic happened. He related, "When I returned, I was surprised by the sight of many trees growing on both sides of the river. Then he said to me, 'This river flows east through the desert into the valley of the Dead Sea. The waters of this stream will make the salty waters of the Dead Sea fresh and pure. There will be swarms of living things wherever the water of this river flows. Fish will abound in the Dead Sea, for its waters will become fresh. Life will flourish wherever this water flows'" (Ezek. 47:7–9). The passage describes an incredible transformation: the desert becomes a garden, fishermen catch fish where the Dead Sea once stood, and fruit trees will bear terrific crops—not just once a year, but in every season. This is a picture of God's miraculous blessing!

None of this happens in a confined space in a building. It happens outside in the culture, in communities, and in relationships. God may be unemployed, but He wants to go to work in the most remarkable, miraculous, supernatural, jaw-dropping way any of us can imagine. He wants to change the world, and He wants us to be His partners!

Today, people are alarmed by all the problems in our country and the world. Sure, there are problems—big ones. But they aren't the end of the story. God is waiting for His people to take Him off the unemployment rolls and put Him to work. He won't do it alone. He works through people...even if He only finds a few people who will take His hand and join Him.

Sometimes I imagine being dead and meeting Jesus. (Yeah, it sounds morbid, but don't wander off.) It could be a plane crash, a car wreck, a heart attack, or old age. It doesn't matter. I envision meeting Jesus and Him saying, "Glen, good to see you. There was a time...Never mind about that. Here's the deal. I want to make you an offer. I'll bring you back to life if you agree to go anywhere I send you, do anything I tell you to do, and speak any words I put in your mouth. Are you up for that?"

I can imagine saying, "Well, God, I'm not in a very good bargaining position, so yeah, I'll take you up on it."

Instantly my lungs fill with air and my heart starts beating again. From that moment I'm no longer my own. I've been bought with a price, brought back from death to life, and given a new purpose for my life. I have nothing to lose and nothing to prove. I never question God's leading, and I gladly do whatever He tells me to do. I'm on borrowed time—no, *redeemed* time. A dead man isn't concerned about his rights, his privileges, or his comfort. Like Paul I can say, "I've been crucified with Christ, and it's no longer I who live but Christ lives in me. All I care about is fulfilling God's will." (See Galatians 2:20.)

Living for Christ is sometimes hard, but living for the devil is excruciating! I know; I've been there. Jesus asks for everything we have, and He gives us back infinitely more. The devil asks for our souls too, but he sucks them dry. Real joy comes from submitting our hearts, our wills, our past, and our dreams to Jesus Christ. Only those who are in the river over their heads and are flowing under the control of the Spirit know what real life is about.

Don't settle for less. Let the Spirit sweep you away.

THINK ABOUT IT...

1. Before you read this chapter, how would you have defined "worship"? How would you define and describe it now?

2. Read Isaiah 54:1–5. Who were the people who received this vision and promise? Why is that important? How does the vision relate to us today?

3. What are the differences between joy and happiness? Whom do you know who radiates authentic joy even in hard times? What kind of impact does this person have on others (and especially on you)?

4. To what extent and in what way is God unemployed in your life?

5. Where are you in the river Ezekiel described? Where do you want to be? What are your hesitations? What about Christ's love, wisdom, and power propels you to take the plunge?

6. What might it look like for you and your church to "leave the building"?

eight

HELP, MY FAMILY IS LOST!

AMILIES. THEY BRING us our greatest joy, and they break our hearts. God has hard-wired us to thrive in close connections with people—especially with the people in our families. We've seen that most people come to Christ through the influence of their most intimate relationships, not from hearing a pastor preach or attending a conference. Closeness, though, cuts two ways. It provides plenty of opportunities for us to display the beauty of Christ to the people we love, but they've also seen us at our worst! Our parents have wiped our rears when we were kids, everybody saw us when we threw tantrums because we didn't get our way, they've watched as we fiercely attacked our siblings for a relatively small offense, and they've wondered what was wrong when we withdrew in sullen silence while the rest of the family had fun together.

They noticed when some of you found excuses to go out with friends instead of staying to do the dishes, and they've heard you ask for money too many times. And some of them have been awakened by the police knocking on the door of your houses because they caught you vandalizing a house in town. (No, not you!)

The point is this: Our parents, siblings, and extended family aren't impressed when we *tell* them we've trusted Jesus as our Savior. They're only impressed when they *see genuine change* in our attitudes and behavior. We may be able to wear a mask of a "nice Christian" outside our homes, but the mask falls off when we walk through the door.

Our family members are looking for the real thing.

AUTHENTIC CHRISTIANITY

For some of us, living an authentic Christian life in front of those who know us best is pretty easy. These families are loving and secure, and people talk openly about all kinds of joys and problems. But a lot of families are more like the Simpsons! Over time, unresolved hurts have built walls between spouses, between parents and kids, and between the kids too. Trust has been violated so many times that people go to one of two extremes: they either trust untrustworthy people because it makes them somehow feel safe, or they refuse to trust anybody and live in a poisonous cloud of suspicion. Of course, many factors and widely varied degrees of hurt and mistrust affect families. Addiction, abuse, and abandonment are just the most obvious, but many families spend a lot of their energies hiding these problems from the outside world—and even from each other.

To the extent that a family endures unforgiven offenses, unhealed hurts, and broken trust, each family member's goal shifts from love to self-protection. When the goal shifts, people play a variety of roles to limit their exposure, shift the blame, and win applause. In these roles they hide behind masks because they're afraid of being authentic—and after a while, they don't even know who they really are any more. Some of the most common roles are:

- The CDP—this is the "compulsive dysfunctional person," the one whose problems dominate the family and distort all interactions.

- The fixer—this person gets her identity from being indispensable. She jumps in to help someone escape problems, eliminates consequences of his behavior, and defends him to anyone who suspects he's not responsible and good.

- The volcano—from time to time this person blows up in rage and uncontrolled anger. He doesn't have to do it very often for the message to be clear: "Don't mess with me, or I'll explode!" People live in fear that it might happen at any time.

- The mascot—to relieve tension in the family, this person tries to be lighthearted. In fact, as the stress gets more intense, the mascot is more intentional about cracking jokes to ease the tension.

- The hero or princess—to gain some sense of value and praise, a family member may try to earn applause in academics, business, sports, beauty, or in some other way.

This is an attempt to say, "Look at me! I'm worthwhile!"

- The scapegoat—people in these families don't know how to resolve all the hurt, fear, and anger they feel. They don't think they can talk to anyone who actually hurt them, so they lay all the blame on a particular person: the scapegoat.

- The closet child—a family member may feel so thoroughly threatened that she retreats into an emotional shell. She may be in the room, but her heart remains walled off from everyone. Or more likely, she finds any excuse to leave the tense environment and hide—in the next room or maybe in the next state.[1]

What does all this have to do with sharing the beauty of Christ with people around us? It's the normal context for many, many people who are reading this book. It's what they live with every day, and it defines the struggle they face to be light and salt in their families. God isn't shocked to learn that many of us come from shattered and strained homes. Jesus came to people like us...people who don't have it all together...those who desperately need the love of God to heal our wounds and transform our lives. I've described these roles so we can repent more effectively. If we can't identify the dysfunctional role we play, we can't say, "I finally see how I've been acting! I need God's grace and power to take steps to change!" As we saw earlier, we change as God gives us insight to "change clothes"—by the wisdom, love, and strength of God we *take off* old attitudes and habits, and we *put on* new insights, new behaviors, and new ways of relating to the people around us. Gradually (or sometimes quickly) we stop playing those roles. We find the radical security of being loved by the God of glory, and we live out our new identity as His bride, children, and partners.

Some people are thinking, "Brother, you're dreaming! You must not have been at our house last Thanksgiving. It was a disaster then, and it'll always be a disaster."

Wrong. God is in the business of transforming lives. Nothing is too difficult for Him! The Spirit of God delights to do the impossible. If your family is impossible, you qualify for a miracle of grace. Get ready. It's coming. Trust Him to make you beautiful. Don't get me wrong. I'm not claiming that God will change your family members and make them more honest, loving, and trustworthy. I'm claiming that God will change *you* to make you more humble and secure, less defiant and self-protective, and more willing to reach out to show love—even to those who have hurt you. I'm not asking you to go back into an abusive relationship. That would be stupid. But God may want you to initiate a process of truth, forgiveness, and reconciliation that might—just might—make a difference in the lives of people in your family. Even if they don't repent, you'll know you've been beautiful, and that's all God asks of you. In every aspect of evangelism we share Christ's love in the power of the Spirit and leave the results to God. That's true no less in our families than in our relationships with anyone else.

When the love of Jesus thrills our hearts, we naturally think of the people in our families and long for them to know Him too. Some of us barge in the door as soon as we're saved and tell everybody they need to get saved too! That's my style, but I don't recommend it. I suggest you casually tell them about your new faith, but don't push. Over the next few weeks and months they'll be watching you like a hawk. If they see the fruit of a changed life, they'll be far more open to hear the rest of your story— and maybe even respond to the gospel. But if they don't see change—not perfection, but genuine change—your words will sound like an infomercial at two o'clock in the morning: dull, meaningless, and unconvincing.

Today people are far more mobile than they've ever been in any other culture the world has ever known. Even a generation or two ago most people grew up, got married, had kids, and died within a few miles (or a few feet) from their parents and grandparents. No more. The Pew Research Center states that only 37 percent of people live in the town where they grew up.[2] The average American moves seven times, and each time the fabric of relationships is ripped and has to be restitched again. Also, broken and blended families are far more common, and many people choose not to marry—at least for a long time. The median age of marriage for men and women continues to rise.[3] Some of those who have chosen not to marry are single moms who are doing their best to provide a stable home for their kids. In our society, "family" has come to have a much wider meaning. For this reason the roles people play today may function in relationships that aren't connected by DNA because these relationships form surrogate families—at work, with friends, and in neighborhoods far from the rest of their natural family members.

In every kind of family God is ready to bring in a

harvest of souls. In some of them He has to do a lot more plowing, watering, and weeding, but He can turn salt wastes into fertile ground. In the last chapter we noticed that it's absurd to think of God being unemployed and knocking on our doors looking for an opportunity to work, but He's a gentleman. He never imposes Himself on us—at least not until judgment day. That's a different story! But God is also a farmer, and it's just as insane to think of Him looking over a field that has no harvest. In a famous parable Jesus described four types of soil, but only one produced a bountiful harvest. In the others the seed of the gospel was eaten by Satan, died in the hot sun of adversity after it sprouted, or was choked out by worry and greed. God uses us to plant the seed of the gospel in the lives of people we love, but we can't make it grow.

The Harvest

Harvest is a time of great celebration. One of the biggest feasts in the Hebrew calendar was the Feast of Booths, which was celebrated in the fall when farmers harvested their crops. Psalm 104 is a long and lovely poem about God's creative genius and the gift of a huge harvest. God gives every part of it: the earth and sun in their seasons, the rain to water the earth, and the crops themselves. The poet concludes:

> When you give them your breath, life is created,
>   and you renew the face of the earth.
> May the glory of the LORD continue forever!
>   The LORD takes pleasure in all he has made!
> The earth trembles at his glance;
>   the mountains smoke at his touch.

I will sing to the LORD as long as I live.
    I will praise my God to my last breath!
May all my thoughts be pleasing to him,
    for I rejoice in the LORD.
Let all sinners vanish from the face of the earth;
    let the wicked disappear forever.
Let all that I am praise the LORD.
Praise the LORD!

—PSALM 104:30–35

You might say, "That's cool. It's good for a farm or a business to do well and provide for a family." But praise for a harvest goes beyond kernels of wheat and slabs of mutton. When the disciples came back from their mission to tell people about Jesus and His kingdom, they told him about the incredible ways God had used them to change lives. Jesus erupted in praise (using words that sound a lot like the psalmist's joy over the harvest):

"Yes," he told them, "I saw Satan fall from heaven like lightning! Look, I have given you authority over all the power of the enemy, and you can walk among snakes and scorpions and crush them. Nothing will injure you. But don't rejoice because evil spirits obey you; rejoice because your names are registered in heaven." At the same time Jesus was filled with the joy of the Holy Spirit, and he said, "O Father, Lord of heaven and earth, thank you for hiding these things from those who think themselves wise and clever, and for revealing them to the childlike. Yes, Father, it pleased you to do it this way."

—LUKE 10:18–21

Jesus was thrilled with the harvest of souls that was the result of the demonstration of grace and power. And who demonstrated this grace and power? The disciples who had become beautiful by being with Jesus.

In too many churches and too many hearts today there's no celebration, no joy, no thrill, no gratitude—because there's little or no harvest. People are singing, but their hearts aren't in it. They're sitting while the pastor is preaching, but their minds are drifting to something else. They may smile and clap, but it's just a show. It's more like a funeral than a celebration! Church isn't about the music or the preaching, the building or the programs. The church is about leaving the building and getting outside into the culture. It begins at home. That's where the harvest happens, and that's what produces real joy.

When God's people become beautiful, family members notice, and a lot of them want in. These people become part of a bountiful harvest. Show me a church without a harvest, and I'll show you a church with no joy. These three—beauty, harvest, and joy—are inseparable. And all three begin at home: parents with their kids, children with their parents, brothers and sisters sharing the love of Jesus with each other and living it out in the fruit of the Spirit. A lot of church leaders and members think evangelism is the pastor's job. I've seen pictures of people gathered around a school of fish. They beat the water and make noise to drive the fish toward a guy with a huge net. When the school is close enough,

> The church is about leaving the building and getting outside into the culture.

he casts it over them. A lot of people think this image

accurately describes evangelism. It doesn't. God has called all of us to be "fishers of men," not "beaters of the water." We don't have to be professional evangelists or pastors to fish for people's souls. Every believer has that responsibility and privilege. We begin under our own roofs.

Some might say, "Glen, that's a great concept, but you've never met my family. They're weird [or evil or stupid or whatever derogatory word you want to put there]." I'm not arguing in defense of their moral integrity or mental sanity. But I'm asking us to look at the Gospels to see what kind of people flocked to Jesus. The good people? No. The clean, smart, pure, noble, and righteous? No. The ones who came in droves were the forgotten people, the ones who didn't fit the mold, those who didn't measure up—the ones the religious leaders couldn't stand!

If your family is at the bottom of the barrel, they're good candidates to understand and embrace the grace of God. But there's another thing: before you bad-mouth your family, you'd better look in the mirror. You're not so hot yourself! You needed God's saving grace, didn't you? You need His love and power today, don't you? OK, then. I'm glad we got that straight. We make a huge mistake— the same one the Pharisees made—when we think we're superior to anybody anywhere. As the old saying goes, "The ground is level at the foot of the cross." As long as we have a checklist of who's acceptable and who isn't, we're just like the religious leaders who gave Jesus fits— and eventually killed Him. Grace makes us different. It makes us beautiful, warm, inclusive, and accepting.

Deborah and I have been part of several churches, and in some of them we wanted to run away and hide. People from the outside looked and said, "What's wrong with those people? They have a cross on their steeple, but they're trying to crucify each other! All we hear about is hatred, gossip, factions, camps, and fighting. Is that what Christianity is about? If it is, no thanks."

Churches don't grow from winning arguments and forcing others to lose, and they don't grow because a gifted pastor brings people in. They grow organically when God's beautiful people go out into the living rooms, offices, fields, and neighborhoods to shine the light of the gospel to their family and friends. We have to *be* good news before we *share* good news. Remember the promise God gave through Ezekiel: "Your fame soon spread throughout the world because of your beauty. I dressed you in my splendor and perfected your beauty" (Ezek. 16:14). Love, integrity, honor, and a servant's heart…that's real beauty, and that's what God is producing in each of us.

THE BEST TRANSLATION OF THE BIBLE

We need to remember, though, that we aren't inherently beautiful. Apart from Christ we're dead, ugly, and stinking. Earlier in the passage about beauty Ezekiel described the state of people before they go to God's beauty parlor: "On the day you were born, no one cared about you. Your umbilical cord was not cut, and you were

> "They have a cross on their steeple, but they're trying to crucify each other!"

never washed, rubbed with salt, and wrapped in cloth. No one had the slightest interest in you; no one pitied you or cared for you. On the day you were born, you were unwanted, dumped in a field and left to die" (vv. 4–5). Ouch. Not much chance of winning any beauty contests.

But God didn't leave us in our filth and helplessness. "But I came by and saw you there, helplessly kicking about in your own blood. As you lay there, I said, 'Live!' And I helped you to thrive like a plant in the field. You grew up and became a beautiful jewel" (vv. 6–7). But that's not all. God invested everything in making her gorgeous, secure, and loved. God explained through the prophet:

> We have to *be* good news before we *share* good news.

> And when I passed by again, I saw you were old enough for love. So I wrapped my cloak around you to cover your nakedness and declared my marriage vows. I made a covenant with you, says the Sovereign LORD, and you became mine. Then I bathed you and washed off your blood, and I rubbed fragrant oils into your skin. I gave you expensive clothing of fine linen and silk, beautifully embroidered, and sandals made of fine goatskin leather. I gave you lovely jewelry, bracelets, and beautiful necklaces, a ring for your nose and earrings for your ears, and a lovely crown for your head. And so you were adorned with gold and silver. Your clothes were made of fine linen and were beautifully embroidered. You ate the finest foods—choice flour, honey, and olive oil—and became more beautiful than ever. You looked like a queen, and so you were!
>
> —EZEKIEL 16:8–13

God promises to let everyone marvel at her beauty.

He's talking about the nation of Israel, which had abandoned God and betrayed Him by pursuing idols—and

He's talking about us, who similarly abandoned Him by chasing after worthless things. God didn't throw us aside in anger. He captured our hearts, showered us with love and attention and riches, and made us beautiful.

How can we respond to someone who has done so much for those who deserve only wrath? We fall at His feet in gratitude, and we shout for joy in His love! He has taken us from rubbish to royalty, from being cranks to become queens. Don't get it backward. He doesn't love us because we're beautiful. We're beautiful because He loves us.

It's odd that Americans are so enamored with royalty in other countries. Every time the queen of England and her family are on television, people can't get enough of them. It's the same way when God turns us into royalty—people can't get enough of looking at us! Kings, queens, and princes of the nations may feel arrogant because they hold their positions by birth and lineage, but God's people realize it's all because of Jesus. We were helpless and hopeless before we met Him, and now we're princes and princesses. That's our testimony, and that's the source of true humility and gratitude.

Peter explained, "You are a chosen people. You are royal priests, a holy nation, God's very own possession. As a result, you can show others the goodness of God, for he called you out of the darkness into his wonderful light. 'Once you had no identity as a people; now you are God's people. Once you received no mercy; now you have received God's mercy'" (1 Pet. 2:9–10).

People in our families can detect counterfeits, but they're close enough to know when they see the real thing too. When our hearts overflow with God's love, when we're thrilled to be called His own, we change. We overlook little annoyances, we pitch in to help, we give without strings attached, we cry when others suffer, and we truly delight at their good news. We're not perfect. Far from it. But we apologize and ask for forgiveness when we hurt people we love. It's a radical concept, I know. It's the impact of the gospel.

All of this comes from the heart. It can't be faked—at least, not in our families. They can tell if it's real or not. When people come around us and notice the sweet fragrance of Christ in our lives, they want to know more—not more about us, but more about the One who made us beautiful. They want to hear us describe the wonder of His grace, the brilliance of His greatness, and the magnificence of His wisdom and purposes. We don't need to push anything, and we don't need to demand a response. We just let the beauty of Jesus radiate from us and joyfully tell people about Him. Some of us remember a poem that goes like this:

> The Gospels of Matthew, Mark, Luke, and John
> > are told by more than a few,
> but the gospel most talked about
> > is the gospel according to you.

A friend asked a teenage boy, "What translation of the Bible is the best?"

He quickly answered, "My mom."

The world doesn't need another sermon. It doesn't need more finely tuned outreach strategies, techniques, and tools. It needs more beautiful believers who are radiant in their love for Jesus. In fact, we need to remember that tools, techniques, and strategies can be helpful, but only in a limited way. Jesus approached people in very different ways, and Paul tailored his approach—not his message, but his approach—to each particular person and group. He was creative, sensitive, and bold. When he met people, he first tried to understand their views, and then he spoke the truth to meet their needs. He explained his approach to the Corinthians:

> A friend asked a teenage boy, "What translation of the Bible is the best?" He quickly answered, "My mom."

> I have become a slave to all people to bring many to Christ. When I was with the Jews, I lived like a Jew to bring Jews to Christ. When I was with those who follow the Jewish law, I too lived under that law. Even though I am not subject to the law, I did this so I could bring to Christ those who are under the law. When I am with the Gentiles who do not follow the Jewish law, I too live apart from that law so I can bring them to Christ. But I do not ignore the law of God; I obey the law of Christ. When I am with those who are weak, I share their weakness, for I want to bring the weak to Christ. Yes, I try to find common ground with everyone, doing everything I can to save some. I do everything to spread the Good News and share in its blessings.
>
> —1 CORINTHIANS 9:19–23

What does this mean for us? It means I have a little different approach when I talk to an old Cajun from Louisiana than I'd have with a teenage surfer I meet on the beach in California. Sometimes I speak to football teams, and sometimes I meet with prisoners. Sometimes I talk to people who are near death, and sometimes I meet college students whose lives are opening in front of them. Whatever it takes, I go, listen, speak, wait, and love them until they embrace Jesus or we part as friends. They don't have to agree with me for me to love and accept them, but I want to be crystal clear. Truth and grace—both are essential. Satan has blinded the minds of the unbelieving, but he didn't blind the heart. My God-given task is to share the beauty of Jesus in an appropriate way out of a heart that is aflame with love for Him.

Quite often God leads us to people at a point of need in their lives. Jesus's parable of the good Samaritan describes two responses to a person with a problem. A Jewish man traveling a dangerous road from Jerusalem to Jericho was robbed, beaten, and left for dead. Two religious leaders, a priest and a Levite, came by, but they refused to help him. They walked on by. A Samaritan came along and cared for the man. He didn't just say he'd call 911. He bandaged the man's wounds, put him on his donkey, and took him to an inn. He paid the innkeeper for the man's lodging and offered to pay any other costs. When He finished the story, Jesus asked, "Now which of these three would you say was a neighbor to the man who was attacked by bandits?" The man listening to the story replied, "The one who showed him mercy." Jesus answered, "Yes, now go and do the same" (Luke 10:29–37).

> Satan has blinded the minds of the unbelieving, but he didn't blind the heart.

In our homes we can always find excuses for not helping people in need—especially people in our families: "They need help all the time." "They're so annoying." "They won't appreciate it." "They'll become dependent on me." And on and on. Jesus is saying, "I'm putting people in your path every day—wounded people, lost people, confused people, addicted people, old people, sick people, unemployed people, stressed people, hurting people, angry people." The priest and the Levite were the beaten man's countrymen. They were like family, but they found excuses to ignore his pain. The Jews despised Samaritans. This Samaritan was an outsider the Jewish man would never have allowed to touch him—until he was broken, bleeding, and desperate. There are people in our lives like every person in this drama: hurting people, those who know better but make excuses, and those who go out of their way to care. Be like the Samaritan. Stop and care.

Jesus's life was all about meeting the needs of people He met. He wasn't absorbed in acquiring stuff or gaining positions and applause. He was totally secure in the Father's love, and He was completely devoted to the Father's purposes. When Jesus floods our hearts with His presence, power, and purposes, we'll become a little more like Him.

Becoming beautiful can feel pretty awkward at first. When I was a boy, I loved to hang out with my mother's mom. We called her Maw Maw Leger. She was about an inch shy of five feet tall, but every ounce was full of love. One of my earliest memories was of her holding me as she rocked on the big swing on her front porch. We had a big family, and everybody loved to drink and party. I wasn't sure when Mardi Gras began and ended because every weekend seemed like a huge party to me. No one in our family was a Christian, and they weren't even religious. They were hard-drinking, hard-living, loud-talking people who were radically committed to having a good time. And man, they knew how to cook—crawfish, jambalaya, *ètouffée*, shrimp, barbeque, and everything else Cajuns love.

They were so proud of me when I played football in high school, and when Louisiana Tech won two national championships, they had a permanent smile! Then ol' Glen got saved, and in fact, God didn't dab on a little salvation. He poured it on! Suddenly I stopped drinking and cursing. My family thought I'd become a victim of alien body snatchers. They thought I'd gotten weird, and to be honest, they were embarrassed. They didn't know what to do with me anymore. At family gatherings they tried to avoid conversations and eye contact. I felt a bit isolated and misunderstood.

A few years later Maw Maw Leger was diagnosed with cancer. It progressed, and her doctors put her in the hospital. By this time she was getting old. Our family was very emotional about losing her. One night the Lord told me to drive to New Orleans from Baton Rouge to see her in the hospital. I knew she wasn't saved. She had never owned a Bible and didn't know any Bible verses that weren't on bumper stickers or highway overpasses. God told me to pray for her healing.

When I got to the room, some other family members were there holding vigil. I greeted them, and after a few minutes I told them I wanted to talk with Maw Maw alone. They walked down the hall, and I turned to my grandmother. She smiled, "Ahh, Glen. I'm so glad to see you."

I wanted to tell her to get saved, but I knew she wouldn't understand what I was talking about. She'd have said, "Oh, Glen, that's nice. It's so sweet of you to come. Have you been doing good? You're such a nice boy."

I wanted to say, "Maw Maw, you need to accept Jesus as your Savior. You need to confess with your mouth and believe in your heart so you'll get saved. I want you in heaven with me. Maw Maw, you have to ask Jesus to forgive your sins."

She would have said, "That's so sweet. I don't know what you're talking about. I'm not feeling good. The cancer is winning."

We didn't have that conversation because I knew she wouldn't understand. I leaned over and put my hand on hers. I said, "Maw Maw, I want to pray for you."

She looked up and smiled so sweetly, "Oh, Glen. Anything you want to do is fine with me, son."

I told her, "Maw Maw, I'm going to pray that God will heal you of your cancer."

"That's so sweet."

I grabbed her hand with both of mine, and I asked the God of power and glory to work a miracle of healing in my grandmother's body. When I finished, I looked at her and said, "Maw Maw, God is going to heal you."

She winked, "Well, I hope so, baby. It's so sweet of you to come to see me. You didn't have to drive all this far just to see me, but I'm so glad you did. It's a long way from Baton Rouge. Thank you for coming. You know I love you, Glen. I sure do." I hugged her and walked out. My aunts and cousins went back in.

A couple of days later the doctor called my mother with some news. She called me and tried to tell me, but she was so excited that I couldn't understand what she was saying. I had a good idea, though. She said, "Maw Maw's cancer was gone!"

All my relatives went to see Maw Maw and asked her what in the world happened. She hadn't seemed very clear minded when I was with her that night, but she understood enough. She told them, "Well, sweet Glen came to see me. He took my hand and prayed that Jesus would heal me of my cancer. And that's what happened. That's all I can tell you."

In two short days I had gone from weird to wonderful!

God doesn't always work miracles when people are in need. But actually, yes, He does. Sometimes the miracle is a physical healing or a divine provision, but far more often the miracle is a caring person whose beauty and love represent the surpassing beauty of Jesus.

Yes, we can be that person to the people in our neighborhoods, clubs, and offices, but even more, we can be that person to the people in our families. Those are whom you've been thinking about, right? Sure it is.

THINK ABOUT IT...

1. Is it threatening or thrilling to you to think about talking to your family members about Jesus? Explain your answer.

2. Can you identify any of the roles in your own family? Which one are you? How does each one relate? How do they relate to each other? (Be careful not to say too much if you're in a group.)

3. How would you describe the connection between beauty, joy, and harvest? If there's little harvest, what might we conclude? What's the solution?

4. Does it inspire you to know that you are the best translation of the Bible your family and friends are reading? Explain your answer.

5. Who are some people in need around you these days? What are some excuses for not stepping in to care for them? Are any of these hesitations legitimate? Why or why not?

6. What is one thing you need to put off and put on to be more beautiful to your family? If you do, what can you expect?

nine

OPEN YOUR EYES

H AVE YOU EVER thought of what you might say if you knew you were about to die? History has recorded the last words of many great (and not so great) people. Some of them include:[1]

- Inventor Thomas Edison: "It is very beautiful over there."

- Statesman Winston Churchill: "I'm bored with it all."

- French grammarian Dominique Bouhours: "I am about to—or I'm going to—die; either expression is correct."

- Queen Elizabeth I of England: "All my possessions for a moment of time."

- Writer Walter de la Mare: "Too late for fruit, too soon for flowers."

- Ballerina Anna Pavlova: "Get my swan costume ready."

- Revolutionary "Che" Guevara: "I know you have come to kill me. Shoot, coward! You are only going to kill a man."

- Writer Francois Rabelais: "I owe much; I have nothing; the rest I leave to the poor."

- Actor Edmund Gwenn: "Yes, it's tough, but not as tough as doing comedy."

- Writer O. Henry: "Turn up the lights. I don't want to go home in the dark."

- Writer Oscar Wilde: "Either the wallpaper goes, or I do."

- Lady Diana Spencer: "My God! What's happened?"

- Revolutionary Pancho Villa: "Don't let it end like this. Tell them I said something."

On the night Jesus was betrayed to the Jewish and Roman authorities, He had His last supper with His disciples, and then He led them out to a hillside to have a final talk with them. John gives us a long, full account of what Jesus said that night. The men had followed Him for over three years. They'd heard Him teach on mountainsides, in synagogues, in the temple in Jerusalem, and in homes in countless towns. They'd seen Him heal people, cast out demons, and raise the dead. They sat on the sidelines and cheered as He argued with the hardhearted Pharisees and cold Sadducees. On several occasions He had explained that the Messiah had to die to pay for the sins of mankind—but they really didn't understand what He was saying. But something was different on this night. His words were different...and He was different. At supper He had identified His body and His blood with the Passover when God's people sacrificed little wooly lambs as substitutes for their children. That night in Egypt there was either a dead lamb or a dead child in every home. Freeing the people from slavery in Egypt had taken the most dramatic act of God in history. Now Jesus was saying another dramatic rescue was coming—and this one involved the death of a Lamb too.

That night after supper they sensed Jesus was giving them final instructions. He was going to die. This was it—the last time He would talk to them before He suffered torture and death. He was uttering His last words, and they knew they'd better pay attention. He said a lot of things about the Holy Spirit, conviction, comfort, and the promise of eternal life. But He also gave them very specific instructions:

> Dear children, I will be with you only a little longer. And as I told the Jewish leaders, you will search for me, but you can't come where I'm going. So now I am giving you a new commandment: Love each other. Just as I have loved you, you should love each other. Your love for one another will prove to the world that you are my disciples.
>
> —JOHN 13:33–35

When Jesus said "commandment," they were all ears. For about fifteen centuries the Jewish people had followed the commandments Moses had brought down from the mountain when God wrote on tablets of stone. It was God's holy, divine, authentic Word to them. God's people had cherished those stones and carried them in the ark of the covenant all through the wilderness, into the Promised Land, and then into the temple when it was built hundreds of years later. Nothing was more revered. Nothing was more sacred. Now Jesus was giving them a new commandment, and they'd better understand its importance! He told them to love each other. I can imagine them saying, "Check. Got it. I love lots of people: the cool people, the nice people, the people who root for my team, the people who look like me, believe like me, act like me, and smell like me." (Well, that may be taking it too far.) That's how most of us erect our boundary markers: these people are in; those people are out. But that's not what Jesus was saying; in fact, He was saying just the opposite. He told them to love each other "just as I have loved you." That's a game changer! Jesus loved people who couldn't contribute anything to His program, such as women, children, prostitutes, tax collectors (who were considered to be traitors because they collected taxes for the Roman occupying forces), and foreigners. And He even loved people who hated Him—not just the ones who got on His nerves, but His enemies!

PIERCING THE DARKNESS WITH LOVE

Have you ever been around someone whose love oozed out of every pore? Maybe your grandmother treated you that way, but I'm not talking about blind niceness. I'm talking about someone who knows the very worst about you and still reaches out to embrace you and help you. That kind of love is radical! And people sit up and notice. That's the kind of love Jesus was talking about that night, and the disciples understood it very well.

When we treat each other with that kind of love, it's like a shaft of light piercing the darkness of our homes and communities. It proves that we belong to Him. We're not just playing games. We're not the bride of Frankenstein. We're the lovely bride of Christ.

A lot of people in churches think they're doing really good when they tolerate people who are different from them. They don't stand in the doorway to keep them out, but they don't do much more than give them a seat on Sunday morning. People aren't dumb. They have finely tuned antennae. They can tell if the person sitting near them is glad they've come or if they feel even a little uncomfortable around them. When a group of people doesn't love the way Jesus loves, it isn't a living, breathing body of Christ. It's a hundred boxes of body parts, and pretty soon it stinks!

And of course, some people are in churches where they'd welcome toleration. All they see is bitterness, backbiting, resentment, and accusations. They've seen movies about Christians being thrown to the lions in the Colosseum, but in these churches the Christians are the victims *and* the lions! In these congregations almost anything is a boundary marker to label people as outsiders: the clothes they wear, where they live, how they talk, the schools their kids attend, the cars they drive, the translation of the Bible they carry, and how much they know the Bible (assuming that if you know the Bible more thoroughly, the more snotty you can be toward those who don't).

In the opening chapters of Acts, Luke describes the events and the culture of the early church. It wasn't perfect. It was made up of people like you and me. But the early church was very different from most churches today.

It was vibrant and alive! People expected God to work miracles, to provide for their needs, and to use them to touch the hearts of every person they met. On the first day the Spirit enflamed the 120 believers, this small group swelled to over 3,000, and soon to over 5,000. Was it because they had better programs than the Jews or a bigger, more modern and convenient temple? They didn't have outstanding child care or expanded parking. No, they didn't even have a place of their own, and the only program they had was summarized in one passage: "All the believers devoted themselves to the apostles' teaching, and to fellowship, and to sharing in meals (including the Lord's Supper), and to prayer. A deep sense of awe came over them all, and the apostles performed many miraculous signs and wonders. And all the believers met together in one place and shared everything they had" (Acts 2:42–44).

Their love for each other wasn't limited to convenience. The beauty of Jesus filled their hearts and overflowed to one another and to the community. The citizens of Jerusalem responded as if they were attending a wonderful wedding. Every day they saw beauty and power personified in the lives of the new Christians. The new believers weren't playing games with God. They were so thrilled to have Jesus as their ultimate treasure that earthly treasures were expendable. Here's what happened: "They sold their property and possessions and shared the money with those in need. They worshiped together at the Temple each day, met in homes for the Lord's Supper, and shared their meals with great joy and generosity—all the while praising God and enjoying the goodwill of all the people. And each day the Lord added to their fellowship those who were being saved" (Acts 2:45-47).

Those who were watching exclaimed that the Christians had "turned the world upside down." That's exactly right. The ones who had been on top were down, and thousands who had been down and out were now up at the top of God's list by the grace of Jesus. Those who claimed they could see were actually blind, and the ones who admitted they were blind were given spiritual insight. They followed a mighty King who had become the lowest servant—to serve them! And they couldn't get enough of His love, strength, purpose, and delight.

Sometimes people have the idea that Jesus was, well, kind of plastic, or maybe like the guy in the stained glass window: pleasant but stiff. That's not the way the Gospels depict Him. He was full of emotion: joy, anger, sorrow, tenderness, and the full range of feelings. In the Gospels, though, one emotion is described in the life of Jesus more than any other: compassion. Wherever He went and whomever He met, He cared so deeply that the term used means "his bowels shook."[2] He loved people so passionately and was so moved by their hurts that He internalized their sorrows and pain. Their hurt became His hurt. He often wept as He shook with sorrow, and He spent a lot of time making sure people felt His love.

Even His anger was fueled by His compassion. In a synagogue one Sabbath, Jesus met a man with a crippled hand. The religious leaders watched both men very closely. It was a setup. If Jesus healed him, they planned to accuse Jesus of breaking the law against working on the Sabbath. Jesus asked the man to stand up in front of everyone. Then He said to the leaders, "Does the law permit good deeds on the Sabbath, or is it a day for doing harm? Is this a day to save life or to destroy it?" They refused to answer.

Mark tells us, "He looked around at them angrily and was deeply saddened by their hard hearts. Then he said to the man, 'Hold out your hand.' So the man held out his hand, and it was restored!" (Mark 3:1–5). Jesus's tenderness and compassion for a man who had suffered for years prompted his anger at those who refused to lift a finger to help him. That day the Pharisees saw a miracle, but it didn't make a dent. They joined a plot with their sworn enemies, the followers of the Roman ruler, and planned to kill Jesus.

Somebody might ask, "Did Jesus have boundary markers? Did He have any designation of who's in and who's out?" Well, I guess so. The ones who were in—the ones He loved and died for—include every person on the planet. Martians? I'm not sure, but Billy Graham has said that if there's life on other planets, Jesus Christ is the Lord and Savior of them too.[3] So yes, earthlings, Martians, Klingons, Gazoobians, and every other creature with a soul…Jesus includes them all in this circle of compassion and sacrifice. He's beautiful to them all.

HOW WIDE IS YOUR CIRCLE?

How wide is your circle and mine? Jesus stepped out of the comfort and glory of heaven to come to earth to reach out to us. No one was off limits to Jesus, and many of them found Him to be beautiful beyond words! How far are you and I willing to step out? How much inconvenience are we willing to endure? How many tears are we willing to cry? How much creativity and prayer will we invest in connecting with the hearts of those around us? How much time will we patiently give to make sure people know we really care?

Have you ever thought about the range of responses to Jesus? Many people adored Him and followed Him, some despised Him, and a few people were afraid of Him—but nobody was apathetic about Him. His beauty was astounding, but it was also terribly threatening to those who insisted on remaining in power. When God makes us beautiful, people will respond to us in the same way: some will find Jesus beautiful in us and trust Him too, some will reject Him and us, and some will be confused or afraid. But the beauty of Jesus is so striking that no one will be bored!

Love means making connections, but we need to keep the progression in order. The first connection we make is with the heart of Jesus. Bob Pierce, the founder of World Vision, saw the devastating effects of hunger in the third world. He was so moved by what he saw that he prayed: "Let my heart be broken with the things that break the heart of God."4

Jesus was the most joyous person who ever lived, but He was also the One most moved by the hurts of those around Him. Joy and sorrow, delight and grief—those opposite ends of the emotional spectrum aren't inconsistent for people who are authentic and who genuinely care for others. If we think following rules is what makes it with God, we'll ask Jesus to help us follow them better and make us more successful. We'll find Him *useful*, but we won't see Him as *beautiful*. When His beauty delights us at the deepest parts of our souls, everything changes. We have more joy than we ever imagined, and we cry more than ever too. Our hearts soar in His love, and they break when we see the needs of broken, suffering, hungry, abandoned, and abused people.

To be very real about all this, some of us may not be able to watch the news very often when Jesus captures our hearts. We simply can't watch the devastation and pain caused by violence, earthquakes, rapes, drugs, hurricanes, and all the other calamities so dispassionately described by the news anchors. Let me put it this way: if you can watch the news without the needs of people at least tugging at your heart, you aren't alive yet. You're still a dead body part in the scientist's basement lab.

When our hearts connect with Jesus, it doesn't take long for us to want to connect with people. They need Jesus; we have Jesus.

Sometimes, desperate needs grab our hearts and compel us to step in to meet them, but quite often the people around us aren't dying of hunger, exposure, or disease. They have a desperate need, but it's not a physical one—they're lost and headed to hell. I met a man named Ken. As I often do when I meet people, I asked him, "So, what do you like to do? What are your interests?"

His face beamed, "I enjoy fishing. I love to be out on the water early in the morning as the sun is coming up. It's great to catch a big bass, but even if I don't catch one, it's fantastic just being out there."

Sometimes we have to hunt for a connection point. This one was a huge neon sign! The problem is that I've never been much of a fisherman. I wasn't sure how to tell the difference between a spinning reel and a bait-casting rig. Some people don't care about going to heaven because they can drive over to Bass Pro Shop any day they want to go. To them it's better than heaven! When they walk in, they look around the huge showroom at all the mounted fish and animals (where do they get full-grown moose and elk?), wander through a zillion dollars of merchandise (who buys all that stuff?), and gawk at everything for hours. Not me. My dad wasn't into fishing, so I never picked up the sport. I've gone a few times, but sitting for hours by the water while nothing's happening is like going to a slow-motion funeral. I've also tried deer hunting, but it was even worse. I had to get up in the middle of the night, put on camouflage gear from head to foot, wander out in the dark to a little stand, and sit for hours in the freezing cold. I thought hell was supposed to be hot!

Within minutes of meeting Ken, I knew that the connection point with him was fishing. I said, "Ken, I'd like to go fishing with you sometime."

His eyes lit up and he said, "You want to go? I found a great new spot the other day and came home with an ice chest full of nice fish."

I nodded, "Lots of fish. That's really cool. To be honest, I don't usually catch that many…and usually none at all. So yeah, let's go to your new spot and see what happens."

Then Ken said words that made my blood run cold. "Great. We'll go midnight fishing!"

I wanted to suddenly find an excuse not to go, but it would be a bit too obvious. I tried to smile as I said, "Yeah, that's great. But, uh, don't fish need to sleep?"

He shook his head, so I mumbled, "Midnight fishing…wonderful…can't wait."

Ken told me he'd pick me up just before midnight a few days later. During those days I tried to get sick, I tried to schedule a trip out of town, and I tried to convince myself that I would be incoherent in the middle of the night so I couldn't talk about Jesus. Still I had the nagging thought that if Jesus was willing to step out of heaven and come to earth to die for me, I should be willing to get out of bed and go fishing so I could tell Ken about the beauty of Jesus. That's what I kept telling myself.

Ken picked me up a little before midnight, and we drove to the lake. We got in his boat and left the dock to find his prime, new spot. We got there and quietly glided to a stop. I was glad we were going slowly because I had no idea if we were going to hit a tree, run aground, or go over a dam. It was dark! He rigged up a rod for me, and I cast into the blackness. Then I sat—one o'clock...two o'clock...three o'clock...four o'clock. Nothing. I wanted to say, "See, I told you. Fish aren't awake, and we shouldn't be either!" But I kept my mouth shut...at least the complaining part. I don't know much about how women make connections, but it takes times like the hours Ken and I spent in his boat for men to let down their guard and talk about things that matter. Most men are too busy trying to impress others (or at least trying to avoid looking foolish) to be transparent with each other. But out in the pitch-black darkness with fishing rods in our hands, Ken gradually opened the door of his life's story. He told me about his dad, his career, his marriage, and his kids. He shared his hopes and his fears. I told him my story too, and I was able to tell him what Jesus has done to me, for me, and in me. I didn't have to push, and I didn't feel stressed at all. I knew why I was there. I was fishing, but not for the finned creatures. Ken came to Christ soon after our midnight fishing trip.

Paige is a young woman who became a friend of our daughter Kelli when we lived in Baton Rouge. Paige's dad, Ed, played football at the same high school where I attended, but he was a little older. He got a scholarship to play at Louisiana Tech, but by the time I got there, he had dropped out of school. Years later in Baton Rouge, Paige asked me to reach out to her dad. She said, "You may be the only person he'll listen to because both of you love football."

I wasn't sure of her logic, but I was impressed with her love for her father. I asked, "What does your dad like to do these days? What's his hobby?"

She answered, "Tennis. He loves to play tennis."

I explained, "Well, I've never played the game, but I'll give it a shot." Paige gave me her dad's number, and I called him. I reminded him who I was and explained that his daughter was attending our church. After a few minutes of conversation, I invited him to play tennis.

Ed said, "Great. I'd love to."

I had to say, "Uh, if you don't mind, would you bring an extra racquet?"

There was a pause on the other end of the phone, and then Ed said, "Sure. Are the strings in yours broken?"

"Not exactly." I tried to be evasive.

A few days later we met at his country club. He was decked out in nice tennis clothes and regulation tennis shoes. I was wearing cut off jeans and an old T-shirt. I didn't have tennis shoes, so I wore flip flops. (No kidding. I wore flip flops.) We talked for a minute as we walked on the court. (He was looking at me, and I thought I detected that he was slightly shaking his head. I wonder why.) He handed me his extra racquet. I'm sure he thought I was "Larry the Cable Guy Goes Hawaiian," but I wasn't there to look pretty. To make our match more interesting, I decided to offer a friendly wager: "Hey, Ed, if I beat you today, I want you to sit on the front row of my church this Sunday."

He laughed, "And if I win, my prize is that I don't have to go to church and you'll buy me a steak dinner. Fair enough." He chuckled.

I knew he was laughing *at* me and not *with* me. I turned around and asked God to anoint me the way He anointed David when he faced Goliath. I was going into combat with a borrowed racquet and tennis balls instead of a sling and stones, but it was still a battle.

The match began. I'd played racquetball before, but this was different. I had no idea how to hit a topspin forehand. I didn't even know what topspin was. Still, I gave it all I had. It may not have been the prettiest match in the history of the game, but I was a determined competitor. I was running as fast as I could in flip flops, diving for balls, and stretching to hit anything in reach. Miraculously I beat him six love! He didn't win a single game. Ed was bewildered and amazed at the outcome. To be honest, so was I, but I gave glory to God. My goal, though, wasn't to win a stupid tennis match; it was to win a soul.

The next Sunday I looked out and saw Ed sitting with Paige on the front row at our church. He got saved and filled with the Spirit. He grew like crazy and later became a board member at our church. I had made a connection on his turf (and used his racquet).

Sometimes the connections God wants us to make aren't with pleasant, respectable people like Ken and Ed. Years ago when I was a youth pastor, a frazzled mom dropped off her son at my office one day. She'd had it with her teenager, and she assumed I was the one person who could change her son's life. Seconds after I met Chad, I realized he was the most hateful, foul-mouthed, defiant kid I'd ever met. His dad was an alcoholic who abused him verbally and physically. His mother came to our church, but Chad wouldn't come. When she brought him to my office, the last words she said to me that day were, "Glen, you'd better straighten him up—right now!"

OK, great. After his mom left, I tried everything I knew to connect with him. I asked questions, tried to open doors of conversation, and told him about myself. No response—not even a glance in my direction. He sat there with his arms folded and an angry scowl on his face. Every now and then a random curse word slipped out between his clenched teeth.

I silently prayed, "Lord, You have to help me!"

At that moment Chad noticed a guitar sitting in the corner. He nodded toward the guitar and said, "Hey, is that yours?"

The Angry Bird speaks! I tried to act cool. "Yeah, I've had it awhile."

He asked, "What kind is it?"

"It's a Martin. Do you play?"

Chad nodded. Almost instantly his whole demeanor changed. God had suddenly built a bridge between us, and I was going over it to make the connection. I walked over and picked up the guitar. I handed it to him. He put his left hand on the frets and strummed. I think he was trying to play a C chord, but he was a beginner. After a minute of Chad trying to play, he handed the guitar back to me. I played a little Hendrix, Zeplin, and Clapton.

I told him, "Chad, let's drop all this talk about you straightening up. Come by every week, and I'll teach you how to play the guitar. You don't have to tell your mother that's what we're doing. She'll think I'm hammering you to change. How does that sound?"

He was all over it. God had given me a single common interest with Chad. He came by for several weeks, and I helped him improve from horrible to bad. But he was excited to learn, and I think he even liked me. After a few really good times together, Chad didn't show up for his weekly appointment. I assumed it was a schedule conflict at school or a family issue. I thought it was a bit odd, though, that his mother hadn't called to reschedule the meeting. A few days later she called. She said in almost a whisper, "Pastor Glen, did you hear what happened to Chad?"

"No," I answered. "Is he sick?"

"My husband was drunk. He beat Chad and threw him out of the house."

"Is he OK?"

Her voice cracked. "I'm with him at a hospital in Meridian, Mississippi. He's barely able to talk, but he wants to talk to you. You're the only person who was kind to him when he was so angry." She paused, and then she burst out, "Pastor Glen, the doctor said he doesn't know if he'll make it through the night!" She sobbed and handed the phone to Chad.

He said softly, "Pastor Glen?"

He'd never called me "Pastor" before. I answered, "Yeah, Chad, it's me. How're you doing?"

He strained to speak. "Not too good. I just wanted to tell you how sorry I am for the way I acted when I met you. I was awful, but you didn't seem to mind. You didn't throw me out, and you didn't give up on me—even when

I was at my worst. Pastor Glen, you're the best friend I ever had."

Now I was crying. All I could say was, "Thanks, Chad."

He then said, "I wanted to call to tell you I'm ready to get saved. Would you pray for me right now?"

I could hardly talk, but it didn't matter. Both of us knew what I was praying. Chad got saved as we talked and prayed on the phone, and God gave him a new heart. He lived through the night, and gradually he regained his health. He had a brush with death that turned into the open door to a new life of faith.

I'm convinced that young man got saved—and is living for God today—because the Lord answered my prayer to give me a connection point. Before Chad noticed the guitar in the corner of my office, nothing worked. Satan had blinded the eyes of his heart, and he wanted nothing to do with his parents, God, or me. But Jesus had other plans. The Spirit prompted that angry young man to notice the one thing that could bring us together. I was available, that's all. I didn't do anything special but follow the Lord's lead to begin a conversation about playing the guitar. And then I pushed aside the unseen but very real barrier of the pressure to change. I offered love instead of condemnation. In my office God was working clearly and powerfully, but He wasn't finished with the story. Chad suffered one of the most horrible, traumatic events any person ever endures,

> You and I aren't mannequins draped with wedding dresses in a shop window. We're the actual bride of Christ—radiant in passion and beauty!

but God used even his father's rage to show the contrast between his rejection and God's beautiful love and acceptance.

How do we get this kind of compassion for people around us? We have to lay our heads on God's chest to sense His heartbeat. He's not oblivious to the hurts and hopes of people. He knows, He cares, and He's thrusting caring workers into their lives to share the beauty of Jesus with them. When we put our heads on God's chest, we hear, "I love every one of them. It's not My desire for anyone to perish. They're all precious in My sight. I gave it all to touch them." We listen until God's heart begins to beat in our chests. Then our hearts break for our unsaved family members, friends, neighbors, and people on the other side of the world. All of them are precious to God, and they become precious to us too.

Listen until your heart breaks for them. Listen until your fear of looking foolish evaporates in the warmth of God's overwhelming love—for you and for them. Listen until your excuses sound ridiculous. Listen until your soul cries for both the brokenhearted and the hard-hearted.

You and I aren't mannequins draped with wedding dresses in a shop window. We're the actual bride of Christ—radiant in passion and beauty! Being His beloved isn't just a philosophical principle or a nice concept. It's the central, compelling truth of our lives! The message we share isn't pretty good news, mediocre news, or not-so-bad news. It's the good news that a Savior has come, the King lives, and He has called us to be His own! This isn't a *set of rules* we have to follow to become acceptable; it's a *heart revolution* God accomplishes in us by the amazing power of His Spirit!

I believe God gives us points of connection every day with the people He has put in our lives. Will we ask Him to show them to us? Will we reach out with compassion when He reveals them? People are dying to know Jesus, to be swept off their feet by His love, joy, and strength. They're dying for us to notice their needs, to look beyond their defenses, and love them enough to step into the messiness of their lives with the compassion of Christ.

You may object: "I can't do it. I'm not trained." You don't need training to love people. You just need to be swept away by the beauty of God's magnificent love for you.

You may make excuses: "What if they don't believe what I'm saying?" No problem. Just tell them what God has done for you and let them decide how to respond. No pressure in the least.

You may complain: "I just can't do it. I'm a nobody. You don't know how much of a zero I really am." If you're saved, you're "God's masterpiece…created…anew in Christ Jesus so we can do the good things he planned for us long ago" (Eph. 2:10).

> The message we share isn't pretty good news, mediocre news, or not-so-bad news. It's the good news that a Savior has come, the King lives, and He has called us to be His own!

How do young couples in love talk about each other? Do people have to force them to tell how much they delight in the other? No, of course not. They almost explode with joy in telling people about the one they love! It's the same way with sharing the message of God's love. When we're thrilled with His affection and attention, we can't help but tell others about Him.

The next step for many of us isn't training or techniques or even to identify opportunities to connect with people. The next step is to put our heads on God's chest and listen to His heart.

THINK ABOUT IT...

1. Read John 13:33–35. What do you think it means to love each other the way Jesus loves us? Whom do you know who loves that way? Describe that person's impact on you and others.

2. Read Acts 2:42–47. Imagine what it would have been like to have been there. What do you think you would have noticed? How would you have responded?

3. What are some indicators that show where a person's boundary markers are? Be honest. Where do you draw your boundary markers between those you are willing to show love to and those you prefer to avoid?

4. How does it affect you to realize Jesus often cared so deeply that "his bowels shook" with compassion? What's the connection between this kind of care and a holy anger?

5. Think of five people who need Jesus. What are the interests of each one? How can you use those interests to make meaningful connections with them? When and how will you make these connections?

6. What does it mean to put your head on God's chest and listen to His heart? How has doing this changed you? Or how will doing it change you?

7. Why is it crucial to connect with God's heart before you try to connect with people?

ten

LEAVE THE BUILDING

WHO AM I?"
All of us instinctively ask this question, but not everybody finds satisfying, life-changing answers. If we try to get our security and significance by pleasing people, we live like puppets on the strings of their smiles or frowns. If we attempt to gain a sense of worth by our accomplishments (in academics, business, church, clubs, or physical strength and beauty), we'll always be looking over our shoulders to see if someone is gaining on us. If we give up on life and hide from risks and relationships, we have some sense of security, but it's at the incredibly high price of forfeiting love, wonder, and joy.

There has to be another way…and there is. Throughout this book we've looked at the stunning fact that the King of creation, the Savior of the world, loves us—not *because* we've impressed Him, but *in spite of* all of our faults and flaws. Trying to establish an identity on performance and applause inevitably leads to arrogance when we succeed and shame when we fail. Grace takes us off the treadmill and puts us into the arms of the One whose love never falters and never ends. We have a new source for our identity, a new reason to live, and a new power to make a difference in the lives of people around us.

We belong to the King, our husband. We delight in His strong love, and this relationship revolutionizes everything. We stop relating to Him as a waiter, business vendor, harsh judge, or Santa Claus. We are Jesus's beloved bride, the apple of His eye, the reason He came in the first place!

We relate to the people around us far differently too. We no longer compete to beat them and win points, and we're not slaves to their approval. We're channels of God's love to the people around us, beacons of hope in their darkness. We live in a dirty, messy world. Paul told us, "Live clean, innocent lives as children of God, shining like bright lights in a world full of crooked and perverse people" (Phil. 2:15).

What's our reason for living? To reflect the love and light of Jesus. He told us, "You are the light of the world—like a city on a hilltop that cannot be hidden. No one lights a lamp and then puts it under a basket. Instead, a lamp is placed on a stand, where it gives light to everyone in the house. In the same way, let your good deeds shine out for all to see, so that everyone will praise your heavenly Father" (Matt. 5:14–16).

When Jesus shines through us, people see His beauty because it oozes out of every pore. We become a little more like Him as we love Him more each day. His love, forgiveness, compassion, strength, and joy become our own—and people see it! We don't just shine like stars for an hour on Sunday morning. We shine all day every day, in every situation and in every place. Our love and light aren't confined to a building. In fact, they shine most brightly in the darkness when we've left the building.

God has given me the incredible privilege to spend time with some wonderful people who shine like stars in the night. Let me tell you about some of them.

Deborah

My wife, Deborah, grew up with a generational curse of oppressive fear. When we dated and got married, she seemed very quiet and reserved. Actually I could tell she experienced more anxiety than most people, but I assumed she'd get over it. She didn't. At that time in our lives neither of us understood the biblical concept of strongholds. Every day she endured debilitating fear that shackled her in the darkness of self-doubt and dread of the unknown.

Deborah's father was the carrier of this curse. He felt very uncomfortable around people, so he always tried to find ways to avoid interactions. He lived with this haunting dread every day of his life. The stress was incredibly oppressive. He died when he was only fifty-six years old—I'm sure the cause listed on the death certificate wasn't "generational curse," but it was a major contributing factor. Deborah's dad never faced his fears, so he never took them to the cross. Instead, he passed them down to her... multiplied and magnified, which is often the case in these curses.

Most people experience a little nervousness when they need to stand up in front of an audience to make an announcement or introduce someone. That's not what I'm talking about. On the very rare occasions she agreed to make brief public comments, she stayed awake all night worrying about it and envisioning herself making stupid statements. This wasn't normal—it was demonic. Strongholds aren't mild temptations or small challenges. They are fortresses Satan has established in the hearts and minds of people who feel helpless and trapped.

As a pastor, my calling and passion are connecting with people. When we had people over to our house, Deborah was very sweet and polite, but soon she excused herself because she felt uncomfortable. She explained that she was busy doing something important. She was a pastor's wife, but she felt tremendous anxiety around people! She certainly didn't speak in our worship services, and she didn't volunteer to lead any activities. Those roles were inconceivable to her. Deborah's identity was completely shrouded by the generational curse of insecurity and the fear of rejection. She believed her pervasive anxiety was simply part of her personality, so there was nothing she could do about it. She thought it was a cross God wanted her to carry each day.

Some people might ask, "What's the deal about strongholds? Doesn't everybody have them?" Well, yes and no. All of us have to wrestle with the effects of our sin nature, even after we're believers. This is the struggle Paul described in his letter to the Galatians: "So I say, let the Holy Spirit guide your lives. Then you won't be doing what your sinful nature craves. The sinful nature wants to do evil, which is just the opposite of what the Spirit wants. And the Spirit gives us desires that are the opposite of what the sinful nature desires. These two forces are constantly fighting each other, so you are not free to carry out your good intentions" (Gal. 5:16–17).

These cravings and desires are, in a sense, strongholds, but the kind Deborah endured is categorically different.

Generational curses aren't bumps in the road; they're deep ravines and shattered bridges! They're more evil, more powerful, and more oppressive, and they make people feel more helpless than normal struggles with sin and doubt. They're demonic fortresses erected in a person's mind and heart, and they aren't demolished easily. The fight requires the heavy artillery of God's truth and grace.

One day Deborah read an article and made one of the most important decisions of her life. She concluded, "I can't live this way any longer with generational curses." She realized her struggles weren't normal. Finally she had words to describe the turmoil she had experienced all her life, and she had a solution. She began attacking the stronghold with the Scriptures, "the sword of the Spirit." She memorized many passages and repeated them often to drive them down deep into her heart and mind. Deborah realized this was the fight *of* her life—and *for* her life. A lot of people want others to pray that God would release them from bondage, but they aren't willing to be diligent soldiers who fight every day in the battle for their souls. Deborah became a soldier.

Sometimes God heals people in a dramatic moment, but often He uses a process that involves our tenacity, the Word of God, the power of the Spirit, and the encouragement of Christian friends. For a year Deborah fought and clawed her way out of the generational curse to a firm foundation of God's love, forgiveness, and acceptance. She courageously confronted her deepest fears, and she chose to believe God's truth about Him, about her, and about her situations. At one point she studied the Old Testament story of Deborah. She had a vision of Deborah as a brave warrior on a horse. She realized, "That's who I'm supposed to be!" At the time she was still timid and anxious, but over time she began to see herself more as the strong, valiant, wise Deborah of the Old Testament.

Since childhood, Deborah had been plagued with self-doubts and fears, but she used memorized passages of Scripture to build a new identity as a beloved, cherished, powerful child of God. It was a long struggle, but God worked to give her freedom. God actually uses our pain to draw us closer to Him and to give us compassion for others who struggle with similar problems. That's what happened to Deborah.

About a year after she read the article and began the fight, Deborah felt led to hold a prayer meeting to teach interested people how to fight generational curses. She thought she'd have a handful of people who would come together once a week to learn to pray through passages of Scripture and claim God's powerful truth about their new identity in Christ. A few more people were interested than she envisioned. After persistent prayer continued for years, her prayer meeting has grown to more than fifteen hundred people!

> Sometimes God heals people in a dramatic moment, but often He uses a process that involves our tenacity, the Word of God, the power of the Spirit, and the encouragement of Christian friends.

In these meetings she stands to lead with a beautiful blend of humility and authority. Some people who knew her years ago might say, "Deborah is a completely different person," but that's not exactly true. She's finally free to be the person God created her to be all along. In these prayer meetings people are being set free from generational curses, getting saved, being healed, and finding hope. Deborah has become a strategic leader. She has trained people to pray with others about particular areas of bondage, pain, and need. Through them God is restoring fractured marriages, bringing prodigals home, healing broken and sick bodies, giving direction to those who have lost their way, and providing spiritual discernment to bring insight to difficult situations. And all of this has happened because one terrified, oppressed woman had the courage to fight against demonic strongholds in her life. She realized Jesus's grace makes her beautiful, and she delights in helping others experience His infinite power and love.

DOUG

Doug's father left home when the boy was twelve years old. Without a father's presence, guidance, and love, a root of bitterness grew in Doug's heart. He was a walking time bomb waiting to explode! As soon as he graduated from high school, he joined the US Air Force. There he began drinking heavily to numb the intense pain and anger that never went away. The alcohol, though, did nothing to bandage his loneliness and depression. Getting drunk only made him feel more hopeless and alone. Doug became deeply depressed; he even considered suicide.

At a Red Flag Air Force competition in Las Vegas, he met Shannen, a lovely woman who was different from anyone he had ever met. They enjoyed talking at the event, and they continued their relationship on the phone after the competition. She realized Doug needed Jesus, so she invited him to come to church. That Sunday I told my story, as I did in the first chapter of this book. He later told me, "Everything you said related directly to me!"

Doug came to the altar at the end of the message. Out of all the people at the altar that day, God led me to pray with Doug. He gave his life to Jesus, and God turned his life around. The most amazing transformation was in his demeanor. Depression gave way to immense, unfettered joy! In the past he had avoided people because relationships had brought him so much anguish, but God gave him the gift of compassion for hurting people. This rough, tough, mean, enraged, isolated, military guy has become one of the most tenderhearted persons on the face of the earth. He had always stuffed his emotions because the pain made him feel weak and out of control. When he felt secure in the strong arms of Jesus, he let down his guard, and his emotions returned. Suddenly he cared so deeply about people that tears began to flow. Rage was replaced by kindness and empathy. God miraculously healed Doug's heart toward his father, and they have a strong relationship to this day.

Maybe it's Doug's military background, but this man understands command and authority. When God tells him to do something, he does it. And God seems to delight in having such a transformed servant at His disposal! The Lord often gives Doug directives to speak words of truth and grace to specific people in need, but often he knows

> The most amazing transformation was in his demeanor.

nothing about them. When he's riding down the road and passes a stranded car, God has instructed him to go back and give a word of knowledge to the driver. One day he was sick and had to go to his doctor. When he was in the waiting room, God healed him, so he got up to leave. God stopped him and said, "The reason you're here isn't about you. I want you to give a message from Me to the doctor." God put a word on his heart, and when he went back to see the doctor, he delivered God's message: "God wants you to know that your mother doesn't have cancer."

The doctor was stunned. He asked, "How do you know she's being tested for cancer?"

Doug explained the unexplainable. "Well, I didn't know."

Now the doctor was really confused. He told Doug, "All the signs point to the diagnosis of cancer."

Doug wasn't swayed. He simply said, "All I know is that God told me to tell you that your mom doesn't have cancer." The doctor looked at him as if he wasn't sure what was going on, so Doug continued, "And by the way, I'm fine too. God healed me in your waiting room."

The next Sunday the doctor showed up at our church, looked for Doug, and told him, "You're right. The tests showed that my mother doesn't have cancer after all."

God has given Doug two rare qualities: divine discernment and the supernatural ability to feel the pain others suffer. God often gives him insight into the lives of people he has never met, and when he talks to people, they're overwhelmed with his genuine compassion. I would imagine it's the same way hurting, sick, and abandoned people felt when they met Jesus and realized how deeply He connected with their pain. People instinctively trust Doug, and they open their hearts to him and to Jesus. He is one of the greatest soulwinners in our church. It's not because he *explains* the gospel more clearly than anyone else—it's because he so powerfully *embodies* the beauty of Jesus's love and power.

Doug has been gloriously saved, but he has never forgotten where he came from. He remembers the pangs of being abandoned by his father, the senseless rage, dark depression, and utter hopelessness. When he meets hurting people, God filters the truth of their situations through Doug's memories and creates a fresh sense of compassion for them. He identifies with their pain. He was there. He knows what they're thinking and feeling. When they sense how deeply he connects with them, they listen to every word he says. The light of Jesus shines most brilliantly in dark places. Doug has been in those dark places, and God is using him to lead people into His beautiful, wonderful, glorious light!

MICHELL

Michell is the daughter of the leader of a notorious gang in our part of the state. She grew up living the script of *Sons of Anarchy*. Her story is much like the apostle Paul's: in the middle of her rebellion God reached down and saved her. The only life she'd ever known was being in a gang, which means she was always involved in turf wars with other gangs. These aren't clubs. Gangs are vicious, hateful, vengeful people who prove their loyalty by committing unspeakable crimes. When Michell got saved, God showed her an entirely new reason for living. She realized most gang members don't really want to be in gangs, but they don't see any alternatives. God gave her three crucial traits: insight, compassion, and courage.

When people come to Christ, many soon disassociate from their former friends—who could have been open to hear the gospel if the new believers had maintained their connections. Michell didn't abandon her relationships with the gangs. They won't listen to anyone who hasn't been part of their world, but they listen to Michell. She offers them an alternative. She gives them hope in the midst of senseless violence and heartache. She's been where they are, she's done what they're doing, and they know she understands their hopes and fears.

In our community gang violence takes a heavy toll. Gang members are shot to prove a point or for revenge. When someone is killed, Michell is there for the family. When one is shot and injured, she goes to the hospital to care for the victim and the family. But she doesn't stop there. She goes to the gang to talk to them about Jesus. And quite often she visits the shooter and the opposing gang to offer the hope of another way to live—a transformed life based on the love and for-giveness of Jesus Christ. In gang warfare she's an equal opportunity evangelist! She talks their language and knows their hearts. God gives her supernatural protection, and He uses her to transform lives. Not many gang members walk away from a conversation with Michell without giving their lives to Jesus. Our church and others in our area have dozens of tattooed men and women who have found Jesus through Michell's love and courage.

> It's not because he explains the gospel more clearly than anyone else—it's because he so powerfully embodies the beauty of Jesus's love and power.

MICHAEL AND PRISCILLA

Michael and Priscilla were headed toward a divorce. Their relationship had slowly soured over the years. Like many couples, bright hopes on their wedding day eroded in the poisonous cloud of doubt, distrust, and discouragement. Priscilla found out Michael had gotten hooked on pornography. One day Priscilla discovered Michael had another secret sexual sin: adultery. It was the final straw.

Priscilla confronted Michael, and he admitted his sin. She asked him to choose the lifestyle he wanted, and he told her he wanted to become a faithful husband. She was torn by his answer. It would be much easier to run away. The more difficult road was to stay and enter a process to rebuild trust. God impressed her that if Michael was willing, she should be willing too.

At their point of desperate need, Jesus stepped into their lives. Two days after Priscilla found out about the adultery, she attended a prayer meeting. A woman spoke prophetic words about a soldier in battle who had been terribly wounded. The image she described was of a soldier with his intestines exposed by the wound. God spoke to Priscilla, "That soldier is you!" But God wasn't finished speaking to her. He reminded Priscilla of David's victory over the Philistines at Ziklag when David and his army had everything restored to them. God gave her the assurance that He was going to give a great victory and restore their marriage.

Michael and Priscilla began to use the rubble of a ruined marriage to rebuild something beautiful. God led them to the passage in Ephesians 5 where Paul instructed wives to respect their husbands and husbands to love their wives.

This instruction became their guide. Instead of criticizing each other, they began speaking words of affirmation and love. Instead of resenting each other, they built bridges of understanding and trust. Everyone who knew them was amazed. How could this happen? It's simple: Jesus had made them beautiful to each other, and He was making them beautiful to people in the community.

In the middle of this glorious transformation and restoration God began to give Priscilla insight and strength to face a generational curse of fear. It affected every area of her life. Fear caused Priscilla to have a lack of trust toward God and an unwilling heart toward Michael. She began standing on the powerful Word of God, and slowly God's truth and grace gave her freedom, joy, and confidence.

Michael and Priscilla were open to the Spirit's work in their lives. They studied the Bible, read Christian books on marriage, chose to forgive each other, and learned new skills of communication. In addition, they received counseling at the church. Their counselors, CW and Sherry, gave them hope that their relationship could be healed and restored. The entire family, including their two daughters, experienced the transforming presence and power of the Holy Spirit. Michael learned to be a strong, loving priest in their home, Priscilla learned to trust and be submissive, and the girls discovered how to be obedient to their parents in the Lord.

As it always happens, God sends couples to Michael and Priscilla who struggle with the same problems: pornography, adultery, distrust, and bitterness. They received godly counseling, and now they have become counselors in our church. God uses them to show the depths of compassion and the heights of hope to men and women who have given up on each other. God is using them to restore broken marriages and wrecked families. The love of Jesus pours out of them into the lives of people who desperately need understanding, direction, repentance, truth, and new hope for the future. Priscilla remarked, "We love to be a part of snatching couples from the enemy's hand and watching God touch, heal, and restore marriages. I used to tell the enemy when I was going through our two-year trial that he was going to pay for what he had done in our marriage—and now it is payback time!"

KELLI

When she was fourteen years old, our daughter Kelli had a dream that God would use her as a nurse to tenderly care for the sick and the injured. By the time she was sixteen, however, she was diagnosed with rheumatoid arthritis. Her dream of being a nurse was shattered, but her dream of getting married and living a normal, happy life also lay in the dust. In her last two years of high school, when other kids are beginning the great adventure of their lives, Kelli parked in the handicapped spot in the school parking lot every day and lived with constant, excruciating pain.

Many nights I sat by her bed and assured her that God's promises are true and right. I often told her, "It's not what you see. It's what He says. If we look only at what we can see, we get discouraged, but God is far bigger than our sight. Sometimes we have to travel a long and difficult road from the promise to the amen." I continued, "Kelli, you need to dream again. Don't give up. Dream again."

Kelli didn't give up on the dream God had given her to be a nurse, but she had no idea what it might look like.

With incredible courage and tenacity, she went to nursing school and graduated. She got a job as a nurse, but the long hours and grueling demands were too much for her disabled body. She had to quit her job, but she didn't quit on the dream of God using her in big ways. She dreamed again.

Kelli realized God could use her to touch the physical, emotional, and relational wounds of people in our community. She came to me one day and announced, "Dad, I want to have a body, soul, and spirit ministry." She put a curriculum together, trained table leaders, shot videos, and began a ministry called Change of Heart. God has used this ministry to transform thousands of people—from first-time visitors to church board members. Satan tried to kill her dream and block her God-given vision, but God used Kelli's broken body and full heart to create a new ministry to change countless lives.

In the ancient world messengers delivered news in person to communities throughout the nation. In times of war and tension the people waited anxiously for these messengers to arrive. They wanted to hear good news of victory, peace, happiness, and rescue. I can imagine people wanting to grab those messengers and give them a big kiss when they got that kind of news! It's the same with us. We are the messengers, and our feet carry us to deliver the best news

> The amazing thing—the pinnacle of grace—is that God uses the raw materials of hurt, anger, fear, addiction, greed, and all other hang-ups and sins in His restoration project.

anyone has ever heard! Isaiah said our feet are gorgeous: "How beautiful on the mountains are the feet of the messenger who brings good news, the good news of peace and salvation, the news that the God of Israel reigns!" (Isa. 52:7). The people I've described in this chapter have beautiful feet, lovely voices, and wonderful messages.

These are just a few of many, many stories I could tell about people whose beauty has "spread throughout the world" because the splendor God bestowed on them "perfected their beauty." I feel like John at the end of his Gospel. He described many important events and messages in the life of Jesus, but at the end he wrote, "Jesus also did many other things. If they were all written down, I suppose the whole world could not contain the books that would be written" (John 21:25). If I wrote about all the people who have become beautiful, this would be a really long book!

God doesn't make nice, pretty, sweet people into splendors of beauty. He takes fearful people like Deborah, depressed and angry people like Doug, gangsters like Michell, bitter and estranged people like Michael and Priscilla, and people with shattered dreams like Kelli. Do you meet similar qualifications?

> We aren't the light of the church; we're the light of the world!

God is in the restoration business. When we restore a piece of furniture, we take something broken and ugly and turn it into something lovely. That's what God is doing with people like you and me. The amazing thing—the pinnacle of grace—is that God uses the raw materials of hurt, anger, fear, addiction, greed, and all other hang-ups and sins in His restoration project.

We don't need to hide these raw materials. In the paradox of faith they become the source of true humility and spiritual strength. In his book *The Healing Path* Dan Allender observed:

> If we fail to anticipate thoughtfully how we will respond to the harm of living in a fallen world, the pain may be for naught. It will either numb or destroy us rather than refine and even bless us....Healing in this life is not the resolution of our past; it is the use of our past to draw us into deeper relationship with God and His purposes for our lives.[1]

And His purpose is to make us beautiful.

When Jesus makes us beautiful by His grace, we can't hold it in. We don't put our light under the bed or in a box. We let it shine for everyone to see! In fact, we can't stop it from shining. The love and light of Jesus become our new identity, our source of strength and purpose, the reason we get up each day.

Jay Leno has a whole fleet of beautifully restored cars. He keeps them carefully stored in a garage. He seldom drives them, so few people ever see them. That's not a picture of us. God has beautifully restored us, but not so we can sit in a garage every Sunday morning. God doesn't make us beautiful only for each other. We aren't the light of the church; we're the light of the world! Desperate people are looking at us to see if Jesus is real. We shine in their darkness, and we shine even more brightly because they can tell we don't look down on them because they have problems. We genuinely care because we've been there. We're restored, but we never forget what it was like to be broken.

Have you left the building? Are you living "Christianity to go"? Are you ready to shine? In our families and our communities we reflect the beauty of Jesus. God wants to point to us and say, "Look what I've done with him, with her, and with them! They were so ugly in resentment, doubt, and sin, but I've restored them. No, they aren't perfect yet, but someday they will be. Even now they're radiant. Look at their beauty! I'm so proud they're Mine!"

THINK ABOUT IT...

1. When we realize Jesus makes us beautiful by His grace, how does it change how we relate to Him, and how does it change how we relate to other people?

2. Which of the stories in this chapter connect with your heart? Explain your answer.

3. What are the three or four most important truths you've learned from this book?

4. How has God been using these truths to transform your life?

5. Read Ezekiel 16:14 again. What will it look like a month from now, a year from now, and ten years from now if this becomes a reality in your life?

USING *CHRISTIANITY TO GO* IN GROUPS AND CLASSES

THIS BOOK IS designed for individual study, small groups, and classes. The best way to absorb and apply these principles is for each person to individually study and answer the questions at the end of each chapter and then to discuss them in either a class or a group environment.

Each chapter's questions are designed to promote reflection, application, and discussion. Order enough copies of the book for everyone to have a copy. For couples, encourage both to have their own book so they can record their individual reflections.

A recommended schedule for a small group or class might be:

- Week 1: Introduce the material. As a group leader tell your story, share your hopes for the group, and provide books for each person. Encourage people to read the assigned chapter each week and answer the questions.

- Weeks 2–11: Each week introduce the topic
  for the week and share a story of how God
  has used the principles in your life. In small
  groups, lead people through a discussion
  of the questions at the end of the chapter.
  In classes, teach the principles in each
  chapter, use personal illustrations, and invite
  discussion.

PERSONALIZE EACH LESSON

Don't feel pressured to cover every question in your group discussions. Pick out three or four that had the biggest impact on you and focus on those, or ask people in the group to share their responses to the questions that meant the most to them that week.

Make sure you personalize the principles and applications. At least once in each group meeting add your own story to illustrate a particular point.

Make the Scriptures come alive. Far too often we read the Bible like it's a phone book, with little or no emotion. Paint a vivid picture for people. Provide insights about the context of people's encounters with God, and help people in your class or group sense the emotions of specific people in each scene.

FOCUS ON APPLICATION

The questions at the end of each chapter and your encouragement to group members to be authentic will help your group take big steps to apply the principles they're learning. Share how you are applying the principles in particular chapters each week, and encourage them to take steps of growth too.

THREE TYPES OF QUESTIONS

If you have led groups for a few years, you already understand the importance of using open questions to stimulate discussion. Three types of questions are *limiting, leading,* and *open.* Many of the questions at the end of each lesson are open questions.

Limiting questions focus on an obvious answer, such as, "What does Jesus call Himself in John 10:11?" These don't stimulate reflection or discussion. If you want to use questions like this, follow them with thought-provoking, open questions.

Leading questions require the listener to guess what the leader has in mind, such as, "Why did Jesus use the metaphor of a shepherd in John 10?" (He was probably alluding to a passage in Ezekiel, but many people don't know that.) The teacher who asks a leading question has a definite answer in mind. Instead of asking this kind of question, you should just teach the point and perhaps ask an open question about the point you have made.

Open questions usually don't have right or wrong answers. They stimulate thinking, and they are far less threatening because the person answering doesn't risk ridicule for being wrong. These questions often begin with "Why do you think...?" or "What are some reasons that...?" or "How would you have felt in that situation?"

PREPARATION

As you prepare to teach this material in a group or class, consider these steps:

1. Carefully and thoughtfully read the book. Make notes, highlight key sections, quotes, or stories, and complete the reflection section at the end of each day's chapter. This will familiarize you with the entire scope of the content.

2. As you prepare for each week's class or group, read the corresponding chapter again and make additional notes.

3. Tailor the amount of content to the time allotted. You won't have time to cover all the questions, so pick the ones that are most pertinent.

4. Add your own stories to personalize the message and add impact.

5. Before and during your preparation, ask God to give you wisdom, clarity, and power. Trust Him to use your group to change people's lives.

6. Most people will get far more out of the group if they read the chapter and complete the reflection each week. Order books before the group or class begins or after the first week.

NOTES

CHAPTER 3
THE RING AND THE ALTAR

1. "When I Survey the Wondrous Cross" by Isaac Watts. Public domain.

CHAPTER 4
THE BRIDE OF CHRIST

1. C. S. Lewis, "The Weight of Glory," a sermon given in Oxford, England, June 8, 1942, http://www.verber.com/mark/xian/weight-of-glory.pdf (accessed March 15, 2013).

CHAPTER 5
THE BRIDE OF FRANKENSTEIN

1. IMDB.com, "Memorable Quotes for *The Bride of Frankenstein*," http://www.imdb.com/title/tt0026138/quotes (accessed March 15, 2013).
2. Jacques Ellul, *The Technological Society* (Toronto: Alfred A. Knopf, Inc., 1964), excerpted at John Saxton Acker, Department of Humanities, Arts, and Religion, Northern Arizona University, http://jan.ucc.nau.edu/~jsa3/hum355/readings/ellul.htm (accessed March 15, 2013).

CHAPTER 6
THE BEAUTY PARLOR

1. "Yes, I Know" by Anna M. Waterman. Public domain.
2. "Love Divine, All Loves Excelling" by Charles Wesley. Public domain.

CHAPTER 7
WHEN DOES CHURCH START?

1. Melody Shaw, "Putting the Distance Between the Earth and Moon in Perspective," Discovery Lab, Grenada Upper Elementary, Grenada, MS, http://www.melodyshaw.com/files/Solar_System_scale.pdf (accessed March 22, 2013).

CHAPTER 8
HELP, MY FAMILY IS LOST!

1. Particular roles are identified by many different experts who deal with family disruption and manipulation. These are some of the most commonly used.
2. D'Vera Cohn and Rich Morin, "Who Moves? Who Stays Put? Where's Home?", Pew Research Social and Demographic Trends, December 17, 2008, http://www.pewsocialtrends.org/2008/12/17/who-moves-who-stays-put-wheres-home/ (accessed March 25, 2013).
3. Pew Research Center, "The States of Marriage and Divorce," Pew Research Social and Demographic Trends, October 15, 2009, http://www.pewsocialtrends.org/2009/10/15/the-states-of-marriage-and-divorce/ (accessed March 25, 2013).

CHAPTER 9
OPEN YOUR EYES

1. Brain Candy Celebrity Quotes, "Dying Words," http://www.corsinet.com/braincandy/dying.html (accessed March 25, 2013).
2. This observation was made by Pastor B. B. Warfield in his message "The Emotional Life of Our Lord," http://www.monergism.com/thethreshold/articles/onsite/emotionallife.html (accessed March 25, 2013).
3. Larry Jordan, "A Conversation With Billy Graham," *Midwest Today*, January 1997, http://www.midtod.com/9612/billygraham.phtml (accessed March 25, 2013); BillyGraham.org, "Billy Graham's *My Answer*," http://www.billygraham.org/articlepage.asp?articleid=4449 (accessed March 25, 2013).
4. As quoted in Richard Stearns, *The Hole in the Gospel* (Nashville: Thomas Nelson, 2009), 9.

CHAPTER 10
LEAVE THE BUILDING

1. Dan Allender, *The Healing Path* (Colorado Springs, CO: WaterBrook Press, 1999), 5–6.

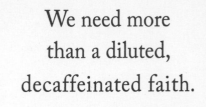

We need more
than a diluted,
decaffeinated faith.

WE NEED
the real thing.

In *Christianity Lite* Glen Berteau
calls us back to the full gospel message:
**Jesus didn't come to make our normal,
selfish, sinful lives a little better.
He came to radically transform
life as we know it.**

For more information
or to contact Glen Berteau,
visit
www.GlenBerteau.com

MORE ME · LESS GOD

Christianity
LITE

STOP DRINKING
A WATERED-DOWN GOSPEL

GLEN BERTEAU